THE Motherhood CLUB
Making a Difference One Kid at a Time
mc

The Busy Mom's
Guide to
Prayer

A GUIDED PRAYER JOURNAL

HOWARD
PUBLISHING CO.

Lisa Whelchel

$\mathcal{L}isa\ \mathcal{W}helchel$ is best known for her role as "Blair" on the long-running television comedy *The Facts of Life.* Now a home-schooling mother, speaker, and pastor's wife, she is the best-selling author of *Creative Correction, The Facts of Life and Other Lessons My Father Taught Me,* and *So, You're Thinking About Homeschooling.* Lisa and her husband, Steve, are the cofounders of MomTime Ministries. They live in Texas with their children Tucker, Haven, and Clancy. www.LisaWhelchel.com

What an honor to dedicate this book
to a couple of prayer warriors,
Reverend Curtis and Reverend Alice Cauble.
Thank you for the venerable heritage you pass down
to Tucker, Haven, and Clancy through your life, prayers,
and son, my wonderful husband, Steven.

Those who are planted in the house of the LORD shall flourish in the
courts of our God. They shall still bear fruit in old age;
they shall be fresh and flourishing.
—Psalm 92:13–14 NKJV

Our purpose at Howard Publishing is to:

- *Increase faith* in the hearts of growing Christians
- *Inspire holiness* in the lives of believers
- *Instill hope* in the hearts of struggling people everywhere

Because He's coming again!

The Busy Mom's Guide to Prayer © 2005 by Lisa Whelchel
All rights reserved. Printed in the United States of America
Published by Howard Publishing Co., Inc.
3117 North 7th Street, West Monroe, Louisiana 71291-2227
www.howardpublishing.com

06 07 08 09 10 11 12 13 14   10 9 8 7 6 5

Edited by Philis Boultinghouse
Interior design by Stephanie D. Walker
Cover design by Cindy Sartain and Stephanie D. Walker
Illustrations by Cindy Sartain

ISBN: 1-58229-438-0

Contents

Contents

Day 9

Day 10

Day 11

Day 12

Contents

Day 13

Day 14

Day 15

Day 16

Day 17

Day 18

Day 19

Day 20

Acknowledgments

Without the help of the following people, I absolutely could not have written *The Busy Mom's Guide to Prayer*!

This has been a remarkably easy and pleasant writing experience. That has everything to do with the genuine and gracious people working at the godly company Howard Publishing. Thank you, Philis, Denny, Chrys, and John. I've loved every minute working with you. (And I believe we had about thirty minutes in all to get this book ready, didn't we?)

Over the last twenty years, Stormie Omartian has played a pivotal role in my life at many transitional moments. Thank you, Stormie, for mentoring a shy girl, frightened wife, overwhelmed mother, and needy friend with the power of prayer.

It doesn't make sense to me why I feel so emotionally connected with friends I've never even met. But I like it! Thank you, Cyber Friends, for joining me on Monday mornings on my Web site for Coffee Talks. You have encouraged me more times than I can enumerate.

I still feel like such "weak sauce" (to use my son's vernacular) when it comes to prayer. I've come to desperately depend on the prompting of the Holy Spirit on other people's hearts. Thank you, Prayer Warriors, who have responded to the call when God has quickened to your hearts that I need supernatural help.

Have I mentioned how much I love Logos Bible Software? I can't even imagine how much time it would have taken me to find almost two hundred scriptures without this phenomenal program. And I had so much fun searching for the buried treasures within God's Word.

Acknowledgments

Thank you, Scott Lindsey and Libronix, for providing more than six hundred Bible resources at my mouse click.

Thanks, Ron, for keeping it fun. You're the man!(-ager)

I can never pass up an opportunity to mention my gorgeous husband and adorable children. Thank you, Steve, Tucker, Haven, and Clancy, for giving me so much to pray about—it keeps me close to my Sweet Jesus. I love you, love you, love you!

Introduction

My heart's desire is to be a woman of prayer, but more often than not, I feel like a failure as a pray-er. As a busy mom, it is sometimes all I can do to cry out to the Lord at sunrise with a quick, "Help me!" before the *son rise*s inside the house and my girls start crying out to me with the same plea.

If I miss my quiet-time window of opportunity in the morning, the shattering of that pane is immediately felt as I realize that there is very little chance for peace and quiet until after everyone is in bed. (That is, of course, after the second drink of water and the third good-night kiss.) By that time I'm typically so exhausted I can barely whisper, "I'm sorry, Lord. I promise to do better tomorrow."

With sincere resolve I begin the next day on my knees covering my family in prayer only to find my wandering mind suddenly thinking thoughts like, "Oh no, we only have crusts left to make sandwiches for lunch." "Did they cancel baseball practice today?" "I can't forget to write a note for this afternoon's orthodontist appointment." "Oh, I'm sorry, Lord, now where were we?"

My prayers are broken into yet again, but this time by an audible voice, "Mom, I can't find my science homework. Where did you put it?" *Where did I put it? It is your responsibility to keep up with your own* . . . And we're off! Another race against the clock with only seconds to spare for a few "popcorn prayers" shot up to the Lord throughout one more busy day in the life of a mom.

A Busy Mother
—An Understanding Father

I truly believe that God understands this unique season in a mother's life. Thankfully, our heavenly Father looks on the hearts of mothers with compassion and understanding. He is not peering down, shaking His head with a "Tsk, tsk, I guess I'm going to have to give her a miserable day because she didn't get the requisite amount of prayer time logged."

Remembering the merciful character of God has comforted me on many occasions when the enemy has attempted to hammer me with feelings of guilt because I wasn't the prayer warrior I wanted to be. In my estimation I was a "General" in the Lord's army. Not because I had earned the highest ranking for a soldier but because it seemed it was all I could do to find enough time for even general prayers. "Lord, bless my husband today. Help my children in school. Please provide the money we need to pay all of our bills. And help me to be the wife and mother You want me to be. In Jesus's name, amen."

God hears those prayers, and He answers them! But I desperately wanted more. I longed for the time to pray for details like my husband's personal walk with the Lord and his relationships with his coworkers. I wanted to saturate my children in prayer for their future and matters of the heart. I felt guilty for not praying for my pastor and the president. And when I told friends, "I'll pray for you," I really did mean to do just that.

Introduction

I always had the best of intentions to pray for all these things. But you've probably heard the ugly adage, "The pathway to hell is paved with good intentions." I decided I didn't like that saying (even if it did contain a nugget of truth), so I created my own personal prayer binder and titled it *The Pathway to Heaven Is Prayed with Good Intentions.*

Wrapping My World

On individual slips of paper, I wrote down everything and everyone I would ever want to pray for. I came up with around three hundred different prayer concerns, and I organized them into ten categories. By praying for one thing from each category every day, I was able to cover all three hundred prayer needs in one month! I felt like a bona fide prayer warrior.

It felt so good to know that once a month I would cover health for my husband, purity for my children, diet struggles for me, prayers for my friends, relatives, and even Jerusalem. All I needed was ten minutes a day, and I could pray for the world, and more specifically, my world. There were even some days when I got carried away and realized I had been praying for thirty minutes without looking at my watch or refereeing a sibling argument.

This prayer system transformed my own life so much that I couldn't wait to share it with my online friends through my Web site. Over the next few days and months, I received tons of excited e-mails from moms everywhere who were using this method. They shared the joy and peace they experienced, knowing their lives, though busy, were wrapped in prayer.

Miracle Minutes

The Busy Mom's Guide to Prayer is the result of my desire to create a product moms could pick up and immediately jump right into enjoying a fulfilling (full and filling!) life of prayer. All you need is a few minutes a day, five days a week and voila—out with the guilt and in with the power! This book has been adapted from my home-made version to make it versatile enough to fit *your* prayer needs.

You will notice that the book has twenty days of prayer. You can use these twenty days anytime that works best for you, but the idea is that there are prayer guidelines for five days a week for a month. Then when the first month is over, you can do what I do with my prayer guide and start over again. The prayers outlined in this book need to be lifted up over and over again.

Each day has six prayer categories. Each category begins with a *Scripture Inspiration* and a section for *Praying the Word*. I have discovered that it is much easier for me to pray with faith when I can ground my requests in the promises of God. There is an immeasurable dimension of anointing that comes along with lining our words up with the Word of God.

The *Prayer Prompt* can be interpreted two ways. If you can only steal a few minutes to pray while waiting in the carpool lane at school, then *promptly* repeat the suggested prayers and rest easy

Introduction

knowing your concerns are covered. If, on the other hand, you would like to linger on a particular petition then simply use the proposed prayer as a springboard, or *prompt*, to dive into deeper conversation with the Lord.

I have chosen six of the most mom-requested categories. They are *Praise, Self, Husband, Children, Personal Influences,* and *Reaching Beyond.* Beginning on day 1, I have broken each of these down even further into twenty *prayer focuses*—one focus per day.

For instance, on the very first day, in the *Praise* category, you will begin praising the Lord for His holiness. Then, in the *Self* category, you will pray for wisdom; godly priorities in the *Husband* category; future spouse in the *Children* category; the personal needs of your pastor in the *Personal Influences* category; and finally, you'll conclude by lifting up the president of the United States in the *Reaching Beyond* category.

Categorically Speaking

Indulge me for a couple of pages while I share my passion in choosing each of these six categories. I love to begin with *Praise* because it helps to put my prayer requests in perspective. As I exalt the multifaceted, brilliant radiance of the character of God, my concerns become both significant and trivial at the same time. The God of the universe cares enough to ask me to bring my biggest concerns before Him so they can shrink in His presence.

Most moms put everybody else's needs before their own, and yet when it comes to prayer, it is critical that we put our *Self* first. Giving is part of the very makeup of a mother (the foundation, perhaps), but we must remember that we cannot give that which we haven't received. This isn't selfish; it is reality. Our relationship with God affects every other relationship in our lives. This is our chance to go deeper with the Lord than ever before, to know Him intimately. Get brutally honest, take any masks off, and let's ask the Chief Physician to perform an extreme makeover so we can look more like Jesus.

First Peter 3:1 says, "Wives, likewise, be submissive to your own husbands, that even if some do not obey the word, they, without a word may be won by the conduct of their wives" (NKJV). I really have a hard time with that scripture, not the part about submission, the *without a word* phrase. I have so much to say to (and about) my husband if he would only listen to me. Thankfully, God does listen—not to what I say, but to what I pray for my *Husband*. What a gift we can give the men we love when we trust God to impress upon their hearts from the inside-out, rather than trying to change them by applying pressure from the outside-in.

Is there any prayer more readily on our lips than those for our *Children*? I think controlling mothers sometimes get a bad rap. After all, it is only because we care so much. When our kids are little we worry about protecting them from others. Once they hit the teenage years, we worry about protecting them from themselves. Either way, we quickly discover that we can't control everything that

Introduction

happens to our children. But that doesn't mean we can't give it our best shot through prayer. Praying for our children is a constant balancing act between handing them over to the Lord and seizing the best for them in the Spirit. I think we are up to the task, don't you, Mom?

You may be surprised at how many *Personal Influences* touch you on any given day. Think about the people who impact your life: teachers, pastors, coworkers. Now think of the lives you have the power to influence: neighbors, friends, unsaved acquaintances. We have the opportunity to not only reach out to those around us with the love of Jesus but to also leave an eternal impression on them by inviting God's touch on their lives through prayer.

Talking with God really gets fun when we begin *Reaching Beyond* our immediate sphere of influence to include the whole globe. Can you imagine being given the power within your own praying hands to change the world? Tends to make that extra five minutes of sleep a little less essential, doesn't it? What was God thinking when He gave us that much power? Maybe it was, "If My people who are called by My name will humble themselves, and pray and seek My face, and turn from their wicked ways, then I will hear from heaven, and will forgive their sin and heal their land" (2 Chronicles 7:14 NKJV).

Filling in the Blanks

I have chosen the first six categories for you, but remember, this journal is *your* personal journey. (Would that make it a *journey-al*?)

We've left lots of blank lines for your own prayers. Use this space however you feel led. You may want to expand and expound on the pre-existing categories or add new categories of your own. Perhaps you want to leave them open to add random prayer requests that come up along the way. Many of you will have particular prayer needs that you can fill in that are especially close to your heart.

In my own personal prayer journal, I have added prayer focuses for co-laborers, specific aspects of my ministry, and an entire category just to pray for each of my extended family members. I love my friend Philis's idea of interviewing her relatives. When she put together her prayer journal, she called her mother, father, brothers, sisters, nieces, nephews, and in-laws and asked them how she could specifically pray for each one of them.

No matter how somebody feels about God, it is a rare person who will pass up the offer to be prayed for. Take advantage of this open door to their hearts and bring their needs and desires to your heavenly Father on their behalf. Perhaps when He opens those doors and answers their prayers, they will invite Him in.

A List of Prayer Lists

I'm confident you will be able to come up with plenty of ways to personalize this prayer journal. To get your creative juices pumping, here are just a few additional categories and prayer focuses.

- **Your Church**—pastors, building fund, elders, choir, youth, programs, unity, etc.

Introduction

- **Small Group Members**—MOPS, Bible study, home groups, MomTime Friends, etc.

- **Large Ministries**—Focus on the Family, crisis pregnancy centers, Joni & Friends, etc.

- **Churches in the City**—all denominations in your community

- **Neighbors**—each family (by name) on your block or apartment

- **People Who Serve You**—grocery checker, dry cleaner, cashier, hair dresser, mail deliverer, etc.

- **People Who Influence Your Children**—teachers, coaches, bullies, youth workers, etc.

- **Your Calendar**—this day next month, to level the mountains ahead of time, etc.

- **Current Events**—news headlines, weather traumas, victims, unsolved crimes, etc.

Prayer Request List

- **The Sick**—infirm, elderly, hospitalized, diseased, and shut-ins, etc.

- **Prominent Ministers**—Dr. James Dobson, Billy Graham, James Robison, Jack Hayford, etc.

- **Personal Impact**—Beth Moore, Stormie Omartian, Francine Rivers, Elisabeth Elliot, etc.

- **Your Children's Friends and Their Parents**

- **Yours or Your Husband's Coworkers**

- **Unsaved Friends**

- Celebrities/Athletes/Personalities—any whom God puts on your heart
- Political Issues
- Grandchildren
- Blended Families—ex-wives, ex-husbands, stepchildren, stepparents, etc.

Personal Ministry Involvements

- The Needy—poor, persecuted, laborers, defenseless, prisoners, victims of crime, etc.
- Missionaries
- "10/40 Window" Nations
- Patients—Alzheimer's, cancer, coma, diabetes, multiple sclerosis, heart disease, etc.
- Other Religions—Muslims, Scientologists, Atheists, New Age, etc.
- School—principal, teachers, PTA, school board, etc.
- Homeschool Issues—curriculum choices, extra-curricular activities, the teacher! etc.

On Your Knees . . . Get Set . . . Pray

"They shall run and not be weary." Now there is a promise every mother needs to hold on to for dear life. What is the secret to avoiding mom burnout? It is tucked away within the first part of that particular scripture, Isaiah 40:31, "Those who wait on the LORD shall renew their strength" (NKJV).

Introduction

Now that you hold this book in your hands, I think it will be easier to find times of refreshing in your day to wait on the Lord and cast your burdens upon Him. Not because there is anything particularly special about this prayer journal but because sometimes all it takes to dig a little deeper is the right tool. Besides, I know your heart is to be a woman of prayer. And when your heart is in the right place, it is inevitable that the *rest* will follow.

I italicized "rest" because Hebrews 4:10 tells us, "For he who has entered His rest has himself also ceased from his works as God did from His" (NKJV). We don't have to worry when we are confident that God is working on our behalf in response to our prayers. As moms we can run around all day, fall into bed exhausted, and still experience the peace that passes understanding. Where have I heard that phrase before?

Oh yeah, Philippians 4:6–7 NKJV—"Be anxious for nothing, but in everything by prayer and supplication, with thanksgiving, let your requests be made known to God; and the peace of God, which surpasses all understanding, will guard your hearts and minds through Christ Jesus."

Hey, Mom, that's another good promise to hold on to. Let us pray.

Day 1

Praise

☕ **Prayer Focus**—Holiness

📖 **Scripture Inspiration**

There is no one holy like the LORD, indeed there is no one besides You. (1 Samuel 2:2 NASB)

☺ **Praying the Word**

Most Holy Lord, there is no one as wonderful and perfect as You; You are the one God, and no one else even comes close to You.

🌸 **Prayer Prompt**

Thank You for the privilege of joining with the voices of heaven as we cry, "Holy, holy, holy, Lord God Almighty, who was and is and is to come." You are worthy of my complete devotion because You are perfect in goodness and righteousness.

🍵 Prayer Focus _____

📖 Scripture Inspiration

_____

_____

_____

_____

🌀 Praying the Word

_____

_____

_____

_____

_____

_____

🌸 Prayer Prompt

_____

_____

_____

_____

_____

_____

_____

_____

_____

_____

Day 1

Self

☕ **Prayer Focus**—Wisdom

📖 **Scripture Inspiration**

If any of you lacks wisdom, let him ask God, who gives generously to all without reproach, and it will be given him. (James 1:5 ESV)

☉ **Praying the Word**

God, I need wisdom and a lot of it. I know You don't think badly of me when I admit that I don't know what to do. As a matter of fact, You are just waiting for me to ask You for wisdom so You can give me all that I need.

🌸 **Prayer Prompt**

There are times when I simply don't know what to do, where to go, or what to say. I don't want to rely on my own limited ability to figure out what is best. I humbly submit to Your will and ask You to give me Your wisdom. Help me make decisions that align with Your will.

🍵 Prayer Focus _____

📖 Scripture Inspiration

_____
_____
_____
_____

🌀 Praying the Word

_____
_____
_____
_____
_____

🌸 Prayer Prompt

_____
_____
_____
_____
_____
_____
_____
_____
_____

Day 1
Husband

☕ **Prayer Focus**—Priorities

📖 **Scripture Inspiration**

But seek first the kingdom of God and his righteousness, and all these things will be added to you. (Matthew 6:33 ESV)

⊙ Praying the Word

Dear Lord, remind my husband not to worry about the things of this world but to keep his focus on knowing You and obeying You, trusting that You will provide everything we need.

❀ Prayer Prompt

Give my husband an eternal perspective. Open his eyes to see that the only thing we can take with us to heaven is people. Encourage him to invest in our marriage and family, and reveal to him the intangible dividends that are reaped. Remind him that You are ultimately our Provider and You will take care of all our needs. Mostly, give him a hunger and thirst to spend time with You more every day.

🍵 Prayer Focus _____

📖 Scripture Inspiration

_____

_____

_____

_____

⊚ Praying the Word

_____

_____

_____

_____

_____

🌸 Prayer Prompt

_____

_____

_____

_____

_____

_____

_____

_____

_____

_____

Day 1

Children

☕ **Prayer Focus**—Future Spouse

📖 Scripture Inspiration

He who finds a wife finds a good thing and obtains favor from the LORD. (Proverbs 18:22 ESV)

☯ Praying the Word

Dear Lord, I ask You to show favor upon my children and help them to find the spouses You have chosen for them.

✿ Prayer Prompt

Heavenly Father, I lift up my children's future spouses to You and ask that You will guard, protect, and keep them from the evil one and from all impurity. I pray for their parents and ask You to strengthen their marriage so they will be raised in a strong, godly home. Shape and mold them by Your Holy Spirit, and help them to stay on Your path so they may find the destiny You have prepared for their future.

☕ Prayer Focus _____

📖 Scripture Inspiration

_____

_____

_____

_____

🎧 Praying the Word

_____

_____

_____

_____

_____

_____

🌸 Prayer Prompt

_____

_____

_____

_____

_____

_____

_____

_____

_____

_____

Day 1

Personal Influences

☕ **Prayer Focus**–Senior Pastor

📖 **Scripture Inspiration**
Shepherd the flock of God which is among you, serving as over-seers, not by compulsion but willingly, not for dishonest gain but eagerly. (1 Peter 5:2 NKJV)

🎵 **Praying the Word**
Jesus, You are the Chief Shepherd, and I ask You to lead my pastor as he leads our church. Give him fresh excitement and enthusiasm for the work he is called to do.

🌸 **Prayer Prompt**
Thank You, Lord, for my pastor. Please bless his home, marriage, and family. Give him times of refreshing with You so that his words will flow out of power-full times spent in Your Word.

Reaching Beyond

☕ **Prayer Focus**–The President

📖 **Scripture Inspiration**
The king's heart is in the hand of the LORD, like the rivers of water; He turns it wherever He wishes. (Proverbs 21:1 NKJV)

🎵 **Praying the Word**
Dear Lord, hold the heart of our country's leader in Your hand. Channel his thoughts, feelings, and decisions.

🌸 **Prayer Prompt**
Thank You for our president. Protect him and fill him with supernatural wisdom and guidance. Teach him to walk in humility and to seek You for direction and wisdom.

Prayer Focus_____

Scripture Inspiration

_____

_____

Praying the Word

_____

_____

Prayer Prompt

_____

_____

_____

Prayer Focus_____

Scripture Inspiration

_____

_____

Praying the Word

_____

_____

Prayer Prompt

_____

_____

_____

Day 2

Praise

☕ Prayer Focus—Mercy

📖 Scripture Inspiration

Blessed be the God and Father of our Lord Jesus Christ, the Father of mercies and God of all comfort. (2 Corinthians 1:3 NKJV)

☉ Praying the Word

God and Father of our Lord Jesus Christ, You are worthy of worship. We are comforted by You because You have reconciled us through Your Son.

✿ Prayer Prompt

I am so grateful for Your mercy. In my sin I am deserving of judgment, but You have not only redeemed me by the blood of Jesus but You've embraced me and pulled me near. Because of Your mercy, I can come boldly before the throne of grace.

☕ Prayer Focus _____

📖 Scripture Inspiration

_____

_____

_____

_____

☉ Praying the Word

_____

_____

_____

_____

_____

❀ Prayer Prompt

_____

_____

_____

_____

_____

_____

_____

_____

_____

_____

Day 2
Self

☕ **Prayer Focus**—Role as Wife

📖 **Scripture Inspiration**

Therefore, just as the church is subject to Christ, so let the wives be to their own husbands in everything. And let the wife see that she respects her husband. (Ephesians 5:24, 33 ESV)

☺ **Praying the Word**

Dear Jesus, I submit myself to You as my authority. Help me to recognize my husband as the head of our family and to accept his leadership. Help me show my husband the respect that his position in our home deserves.

❀ **Prayer Prompt**

I understand that my respect ministers to my husband even more than my love for him does. Show me how I can build him up and put a guard on my mouth when I'm tempted to tear him down. Love my husband through me, and teach me to enjoy finding ways to serve him throughout the day (and night).

🍵 Prayer Focus_____

📖 Scripture Inspiration

_____
_____
_____
_____

🕉 Praying the Word

_____
_____
_____
_____
_____
_____

🌼 Prayer Prompt

_____
_____
_____
_____
_____
_____
_____
_____
_____
_____

Day 2
Husband

☕ **Prayer Focus**—Daily Devotions

📖 **Scripture Inspiration**

How can a young man keep his way pure? By guarding it according to your word. With my whole heart I seek you; let me not wander from your commandments! (Psalm 119:9–10 ESV)

◎ **Praying the Word**

Put a deep desire in my husband's heart to seek You. Teach him to cling to Your commandments and obey them, for that is how he will remain safe and sinless.

❀ **Prayer Prompt**

Draw my husband closer to You. Give him a hunger and thirst to spend time with You daily. May he look forward to his set time with You to share his heart, unload his burdens, and communicate with You in prayer. Open the Scriptures to him with such a fresh revelation that he can't wait to hear what You want to speak to him every day.

Prayer Focus_____

Scripture Inspiration

_____
_____
_____
_____

Praying the Word

_____
_____
_____
_____
_____

Prayer Prompt

_____
_____
_____
_____
_____
_____
_____
_____
_____
_____
_____

Day 2
Children

☕ **Prayer Focus**—Siblings

📖**Scripture Inspiration**

Finally, all of you be of one mind, having compassion for one another; love as brothers, be tenderhearted, be courteous; not returning evil for evil or reviling for reviling, but on the contrary blessing, knowing that you were called to this, that you may inherit a blessing. (1 Peter 3:8–9 NKJV)

☉ **Praying the Word**

Father, I pray for a blessing on our home. I ask for unity, sincere love for each other, gratefulness for the privilege of siblings, kindness, and sensitivity. I ask You to grant my children self-control not to respond tit-for-tat or add insult to injury, but instead, to overcome evil with good.

❀ **Prayer Prompt**

O Lord, grant peace to this family. May the sweetness of the Holy Spirit permeate every inch of this household. Enable my children to encourage one another, cherish one another, and be quick to forgive and be merciful. Help them to be slow to speak, slow to anger, and willing to listen. Make my children each other's best friends.

☕ Prayer Focus_____

📖 Scripture Inspiration

_____
_____
_____
_____

⟲ Praying the Word

_____
_____
_____
_____
_____
_____

❀ Prayer Prompt

_____
_____
_____
_____
_____
_____
_____
_____
_____

Day 2
Personal Influences

☕ **Prayer Focus**–Youth Pastor

📖 **Scripture Inspiration**
When I was a child, I spoke like a child, I thought like a child, I reasoned like a child. When I became a man, I gave up childish ways. (1 Corinthians 13:11 ESV)

🕊 **Praying the Word**
Guide our youth pastor as he leads our children into young adulthood. Show him how to teach them to leave childish things behind and embrace the responsibilities and privileges of being an adult.

🌸 **Prayer Prompt**
Strengthen our youth pastor's personal relationship with You so he may model true discipleship to his young flock.

Reaching Beyond

☕ **Prayer Focus**–America

📖 **Scripture Inspiration**
If my people . . . pray and seek my face and turn from their wicked ways, then I will hear from heaven and will forgive their sin and heal their land. (2 Chronicles 7:14 ESV)

🕊 **Praying the Word**
We humbly kneel before You with repentant hearts and ask You to forgive our sins and heal our nation.

🌸 **Prayer Prompt**
Thank You for the favor that is upon us. Lead us by Your right hand. God bless America.

☕ Prayer Focus_____

📖 Scripture Inspiration

_____
_____

🌀 Praying the Word

_____
_____

🌸 Prayer Prompt

_____
_____
_____

☕ Prayer Focus_____

📖 Scripture Inspiration

_____
_____

🌀 Praying the Word

_____
_____

🌸 Prayer Prompt

_____
_____
_____

21

Day 3

Praise

☕ **Prayer Focus**—Faithfulness

📖 **Scripture Inspiration**

I will sing of the loving kindness of the Lord forever; To all generations I will make known Your faithfulness with my mouth. (Psalm 89:1 NASB)

⟳ **Praying the Word**

I will sing of Your loving kindness forever, Lord, and I will personally tell everyone about Your faithfulness to me.

✿ **Prayer Prompt**

Even when I don't have any faith, You are still faithful. Your love and commitment never change. You have never let me down in the past, and I know I can trust You for the future. I will rest in You and Your character.

☕ Prayer Focus _____

📖 Scripture Inspiration

_____

_____

_____

_____

🌀 Praying the Word

_____

_____

_____

_____

_____

_____

🌸 Prayer Prompt

_____

_____

_____

_____

_____

_____

_____

_____

_____

_____

Day 3
Self

☕ **Prayer Focus**—Role as Mother

📖 **Scripture Inspiration**

You shall teach them diligently to your children, and shall talk of them when you sit in your house, and when you walk by the way, and when you lie down, and when you rise.
(Deuteronomy 6:7 ESV)

🕑 **Praying the Word**

Dear heavenly Father, write Your Word on my heart so that Your wisdom simply flows from my mouth throughout the day that I might teach my children Your ways.

🌼 **Prayer Prompt**

Thank You for the privilege of being a mother and for the precious gifts You've entrusted to me. Let me begin by giving them back to You; they are safer in Your strong and loving hands. Anoint me to teach, train, and love my children beyond my human capabilities. Make me the mother You've specifically created me to be for these particular children.

Prayer Focus _____

Scripture Inspiration

_____
_____
_____
_____

Praying the Word

_____
_____
_____
_____
_____

Prayer Prompt

_____
_____
_____
_____
_____
_____
_____
_____
_____

Day 3
Husband

☕ **Prayer Focus**—Role as Husband

📖 **Scripture Inspiration**

Husbands, love your wives, as Christ loved the church and gave himself up for her. (Ephesians 5:25 ESV)

☉ **Praying the Word**

Jesus, fill my husband's heart with Your love for me, and show him how to love me with the same kind of sacrificial love You have for him.

🌼 **Prayer Prompt**

I know my husband loves me and he desires to serve me and make me happy. Thank You for that. Make him the husband that he longs to be and that I need. Help me to remember to encourage him as he reaches out to show his love, whether in words or actions. Teach him how to care for me with as much attention as he would show himself.

🍵 Prayer Focus_____

📖 Scripture Inspiration

_____

_____

_____

_____

🌀 Praying the Word

_____

_____

_____

_____

_____

🌸 Prayer Prompt

_____

_____

_____

_____

_____

_____

_____

_____

_____

Day 3
Children

📖**Scripture Inspiration**

The fear of the LORD is the beginning of knowledge, but fools despise wisdom and instruction. (Proverbs 1:7 NKJV)

☺ **Praying the Word**

Lord, grant my children a healthy respect for Your authority. Teach them to love knowledge, seek wisdom, and obey instruction.

🌸 **Prayer Prompt**

Instill in my children a right understanding of the blessing of authority. May they enjoy the safety and protection that comes from submitting to those over them. Give them a teachable spirit that is open to learning from the wisdom of others. Teach them to honor You, their parents, those placed in positions above them, and the elderly.

Prayer Focus_____

Scripture Inspiration

_____

_____

_____

_____

Praying the Word

_____

_____

_____

_____

_____

Prayer Prompt

_____

_____

_____

_____

_____

_____

_____

_____

_____

Day 3

Personal Influences

☕ **Prayer Focus**–Sunday School Teachers

📖 **Scripture Inspiration**
The things that you have heard from me among many witnesses,
commit these to faithful men who will be able to teach others also.
(2 Timothy 2:2 NKJV)

◎ **Praying the Word**
Continue to speak to our Sunday School teachers so they may
faithfully pass on what they are learning from You.

🦋 **Prayer Prompt**
Raise up Sunday School teachers who are called to teach and
disciple adults and love and train children. As they give of themselves, fill them with Your pleasure and our gratitude.

Reaching Beyond

☕ **Prayer Focus**–Governor

📖 **Scripture Inspiration**
Let every soul be subject to the governing authorities. For there is
no authority except from God. (Romans 13:1 NKJV)

◎ **Praying the Word**
Help me to submit to the office of the governor of our state,
knowing that the authority to govern comes from You.

🦋 **Prayer Prompt**
Anoint our governor for the work You've called him to do. Grant
him wisdom, and give Him Your vision for our state and the
courage to see it become a reality.

☕ Prayer Focus_____

📖 Scripture Inspiration

_____

_____

◎ Praying the Word

_____

_____

❀ Prayer Prompt

_____

_____

_____

☕ Prayer Focus_____

📖 Scripture Inspiration

_____

_____

◎ Praying the Word

_____

_____

❀ Prayer Prompt

_____

_____

_____

Day 4

Praise

☕ **Prayer Focus**–Patience

📖 **Scripture Inspiration**

The Lord is not slow to fulfill his promise as some count slowness, but is patient toward you.
(2 Peter 3:9 ESV)

☺ **Praying the Word**

Lord, I know You will fulfill all Your promises in Your perfect timing. Help me to be patient, as You are patient toward me. I trust that any delay I perceive is in reality Your perfect wisdom being acted out on my behalf.

❀ **Prayer Prompt**

I'm so thankful that You are patient and longsuffering with me. I know that You have suffered with me a long time in some areas. Thank You for never giving up on me. I know that You will never leave me or forsake me. Thank You for believing in me and for Your willingness to wait patiently as I slowly become all that You've created me to be.

🍵 Prayer Focus _____

📖 Scripture Inspiration

_____

_____

_____

_____

☯ Praying the Word

_____

_____

_____

_____

_____

🌸 Prayer Prompt

_____

_____

_____

_____

_____

_____

_____

_____

_____

Day 4

Self

☕ **Prayer Focus**—Marriage

📖 **Scripture Inspiration**

For this reason a man shall leave his father and mother and be joined to his wife, and the two shall become one flesh. This is a great mystery, but I speak concerning Christ and the church. (Ephesians 5:31–32 NKJV)

☉ **Praying the Word**

O Creator, enable my husband and me to cling to one another so completely that we are no longer acting as two separate people but as one married couple. As I respectfully submit to my husband and he sacrificially loves me, may the world see Christ's redemption plan through us.

❀ **Prayer Prompt**

Thank You for my marriage—the good, the bad, and the ugly. Continue to refine me and change me through the hard times so that I might look and act more like You. Please bless our marriage and draw us each closer to You and, as a result, closer to each other. Keep us together, and do not let anything separate us. By Your grace make our marriage stronger every day.

🍵 Prayer Focus_____

📖 Scripture Inspiration

_____

_____

_____

_____

🌀 Praying the Word

_____

_____

_____

_____

_____

_____

🌸 Prayer Prompt

_____

_____

_____

_____

_____

_____

_____

_____

_____

_____

Day 4

Husband

☕ **Prayer Focus**—Role as Father

📖 **Scripture Inspiration**

For whom the Lord loves He corrects, just as a father the son in whom he delights. (Proverbs 3:12 NKJV)

⊙ **Praying the Word**

Fill my husband's heart with Your love. Wash over him with fresh joy at the privilege of being a parent. Allow any discipline to flow out of this joy and love.

🌸 **Prayer Prompt**

Encourage my husband as a father. Give him wisdom to lead us as a family. Supply him with all the patience, self-control, gentleness, and courage he needs to be a father in today's world. Work a godly respect for authority in our children's hearts and an unconditional, affectionate, firm love in his heart for them.

🍵 Prayer Focus_____

📖 Scripture Inspiration

_____

_____

_____

_____

⊙ Praying the Word

_____

_____

_____

_____

_____

❀ Prayer Prompt

_____

_____

_____

_____

_____

_____

_____

_____

_____

Day 4

Children

Prayer Focus—Walk with God

Scripture Inspiration

I have no greater joy than to hear that my children walk in truth. (3 John 4 NKJV)

Praying the Word

Dear Jesus, please give me the incomparable joy of knowing that my children are walking with You.

Prayer Prompt

Heavenly Father, instill in my children a love for worship, prayer, and Your Word at an early age. Establish patterns of devotion in them now that will carry through the rest of their lives. Teach them to walk in the Spirit, depend on Your strength, love You with all their hearts, hear Your voice, obey Your commands, and follow hard after You.

Prayer Focus _____

Scripture Inspiration

_____

_____

_____

_____

Praying the Word

_____

_____

_____

_____

_____

Prayer Prompt

_____

_____

_____

_____

_____

_____

_____

_____

_____

Day 4

Personal Influences

☕ **Prayer Focus**–Associate Pastor

📖 **Scripture Inspiration**

Jonathon said to David, "Whatever you say, I will do for you."
(1 Samuel 20:4 ESV)

◎ **Praying the Word**

Anoint our associate pastor to be the armor-bearer for our senior pastor. Give him a ready willingness to serve the vision You have for our church.

🌸 **Prayer Prompt**

Reveal to our associate pastor the important role he plays in our church. Strengthen him to support our senior pastor. Remind us to encourage him, but when we fail, may Your smile of recognition be enough.

Reaching Beyond

☕ **Prayer Focus**–Presidential Advisors

📖 **Scripture Inspiration**

With counsel and wisdom Daniel answered Arioch, the captain of the king's guard. (Daniel 2:14 NKJV)

◎ **Praying the Word**

May the president's advisors offer wise counsel.

🌸 **Prayer Prompt**

Surround the president with good men and women who will boldly counsel him with wisdom from You. May they serve our country by serving our president from a pure heart.

Prayer Focus_____

Scripture Inspiration

_____

_____

Praying the Word

_____

_____

Prayer Prompt

_____

_____

_____

Prayer Focus_____

Scripture Inspiration

_____

_____

Praying the Word

_____

_____

Prayer Prompt

_____

_____

_____

Day 5

Praise

📖 Scripture Inspiration

But the Helper, the Holy Spirit, whom the Father will send in my name, he will teach you all things and bring to your remembrance all that I have said to you. (John 14:26 ESV)

⊙ Praying the Word

Thank You, Father, for sending the Helper, the Holy Spirit, to teach me all things and remind me of everything You have said to me.

🌸 Prayer Prompt

I love the Holy Spirit; thank You for leaving Him here on earth when You went back to heaven. Father, fill me to overflowing with the Holy Spirit, and reveal Jesus to me and through me by His power. I worship You, God the Father, Son, and Holy Spirit.

Prayer Focus _____

Scripture Inspiration

_____
_____
_____
_____

Praying the Word

_____
_____
_____
_____
_____

Prayer Prompt

_____
_____
_____
_____
_____
_____
_____
_____
_____
_____

Day 5

Self

📖 Scripture Inspiration

Death and life are in the power of the tongue, and those who love it will eat its fruits. (Proverbs 18:21 ESV)

☉ Praying the Word

I am aware of the destruction my own tongue can bring and also its power to bring life. My desire is that my words be sweet and satisfying and that they bring health to all those who hear them.

✿ Prayer Prompt

I realize that any word that comes out of my mouth originates in my heart. With that in mind, I ask You to cleanse me from within and fill me with Your Spirit so that I may speak words that bring life. Most of all, may my words be pleasing to You.

☕ Prayer Focus _____

📖 Scripture Inspiration

_____

_____

_____

_____

🕐 Praying the Word

_____

_____

_____

_____

_____

_____

🌸 Prayer Prompt

_____

_____

_____

_____

_____

_____

_____

_____

_____

_____

Day 5
Husband

☕ **Prayer Focus**—Work

📖 **Scripture Inspiration**

Let the favor of the Lord our God be upon us, and establish the work of our hands upon us; yes, establish the work of our hands! (Psalm 90:17 ESV)

☉ **Praying the Word**

God, I pray that not only would Your favor be upon my husband, but that he would also be well-regarded by all those he works for and with. I ask that everything he sets his hand toward would grow and multiply and that he would gain acceptance and recognition for the work You accomplish through him.

🌼 **Prayer Prompt**

I pronounce blessing on my husband's work. I'm asking for provision and favor in every area of his career. Give him a fresh joy for the place You've called him to minister and the work You've ordained for him to do. Give him wisdom and strength to do an excellent job with all of his heart. Remind him that he is ultimately working as unto You, not man.

☕ Prayer Focus_____

📖 Scripture Inspiration

_____
_____
_____
_____

⊙ Praying the Word

_____
_____
_____
_____
_____
_____

❀ Prayer Prompt

_____
_____
_____
_____
_____
_____
_____
_____
_____
_____

47

Day 5
Children

📖 **Scripture Inspiration**

Children, obey your parents in the Lord, for this is right.
(Ephesians 6:1 ESV)

🌀 **Praying the Word**

Lord, teach my children to love righteousness and, out of obedience to You, obey their parents.

🌸 **Prayer Prompt**

Please put a love for obedience in my children's hearts. May they long to do right and feel remorseful when they do wrong. Help me to train them to obey their father and me as their parents so they will follow You without arguing when they are grown. I pray they will develop a habit of complete obedience that comes from a heart that trusts Your Word and wants to please You.

Prayer Focus_____

Scripture Inspiration

_____
_____
_____
_____

Praying the Word

_____
_____
_____
_____
_____
_____

Prayer Prompt

_____
_____
_____
_____
_____
_____
_____
_____
_____
_____

Day 5
Personal Influences

☕ **Prayer Focus**–Church

📖 **Scripture Inspiration**
So the churches were strengthened in the faith, and they increased in numbers daily. (Acts 16:5 ESV)

☾ **Praying the Word**
Build up our church in strong relationships with You and each other and out of that strength draw many people to You.

❀ **Prayer Prompt**
Keep our church living and breathing Your Spirit so there may be unity and vision within the body. Cover all the details that are part of running an organization, and make our church a light to our community.

Reaching Beyond

☕ **Prayer Focus**–Local Government

📖 **Scripture Inspiration**
Choose some men from each tribe who have wisdom, understanding, and a good reputation. (Deuteronomy 1:13 NLT)

☾ **Praying the Word**
Help us to perceive Your will when we vote. May we choose wise, understanding men and women with good reputations.

❀ **Prayer Prompt**
Help us take our privilege to vote seriously by researching the candidates and issues so we can use our influence for righteousness.

🍵 Prayer Focus_____

📖 Scripture Inspiration

_____
_____

☯ Praying the Word

_____
_____

✿ Prayer Prompt

_____
_____
_____

🍵 Prayer Focus_____

📖 Scripture Inspiration

_____
_____

☯ Praying the Word

_____
_____

✿ Prayer Prompt

_____
_____
_____

Day 6

Praise

☕ **Prayer Focus**—Forgiveness

📖 **Scripture Inspiration**

You answered them, O Lord our God; You were to them God-Who-Forgives. (Psalm 99:8 NKJV)

🔄 **Praying the Word**

You have answered me, O Lord, my God of Forgiveness, which is Your very name and character.

❀ **Prayer Prompt**

How can I even begin to thank You for Your forgiveness? Without the sacrifice of Your Son, Jesus, I would be so lost and eaten up with guilt. I am eternally grateful for, not only the forgiveness of my sins, but also Your ongoing forgiveness of my weaknesses and selfishness. Thank You, too, for choosing to forget my sin. I receive the free gift of forgiveness that You give.

Prayer Focus_____

Scripture Inspiration

_____
_____
_____
_____

Praying the Word

_____
_____
_____
_____
_____
_____

Prayer Prompt

_____
_____
_____
_____
_____
_____
_____
_____
_____
_____

Day 6

Self

☕ **Prayer Focus**—Thoughts

📖 **Scripture Inspiration**

Do not be conformed to this world, but be transformed by the renewal of your mind. (Romans 12:2 ESV)

⊚ **Praying the Word**

I do not want to become like the world, and I know that any change begins with my thoughts. Cleanse my mind, and help me to focus on You so that I might become like You.

❀ **Prayer Prompt**

Help me to bring every thought into captivity to the obedience of Christ. When my mind starts to wander down paths that eventually lead to sin, stop me in my tracks so that I might repent and turn around to walk toward You. Remind me to meditate on Your Word when I'm tempted to dwell on negative or sinful thoughts.

☕ Prayer Focus_____

📖 Scripture Inspiration

_____
_____
_____
_____

☾ Praying the Word

_____
_____
_____
_____
_____
_____

❀ Prayer Prompt

_____
_____
_____
_____
_____
_____
_____
_____
_____

Day 6

Husband

☕ **Prayer Focus**—Finances

📖 **Scripture Inspiration**

Be diligent to know the state of your flocks, and attend to your herds, for riches are not forever, nor does a crown endure for all generations. (Proverbs 27: 23–24 NKJV)

☯ **Praying the Word**

Bolster my husband's resolve to pay diligent attention to our finances. Motivate him to look down the road and be ready for the future. Give him wisdom to attend to our future.

🌸 **Prayer Prompt**

Lord, give us peace when it comes to finances. Teach us how to live comfortably with everything You have provided for us. Keep us from spending more than we need, so that stress and division can't find a place within our home. Increase our faith to remember that You are willing and able to supply all of our needs. Thank You for the privilege of giving a portion back to You in tithes and offerings.

Prayer Focus _____

Scripture Inspiration

_____
_____
_____
_____

Praying the Word

_____
_____
_____
_____
_____
_____

Prayer Prompt

_____
_____
_____
_____
_____
_____
_____
_____
_____

Day 6
Children

Prayer Focus—Holiness

Scripture Inspiration

As He who called you is holy, you also be holy in all your conduct, since it is written, "You shall be holy, for I am holy." (1 Peter 1: 15–16 ESV)

Praying the Word

O Holy Lord, because You have called my children unto holiness, I ask You to give them the power to walk in holiness.

Prayer Prompt

Almighty God, I consecrate my children to You and ask that You would set them apart for Your holy purposes. May they love the things that You love and hate the things that You hate. Teach them to run from the kingdom of this world and walk in the kingdom of heaven.

Prayer Focus_____

Scripture Inspiration

_____

_____

_____

_____

Praying the Word

_____

_____

_____

_____

_____

_____

Prayer Prompt

_____

_____

_____

_____

_____

_____

_____

_____

_____

_____

Day 6

Personal Influences

☕ **Prayer Focus**–Friends

📖 **Scripture Inspiration**

As iron sharpens iron, a friend sharpens a friend.
(Proverbs 27:17 NLT)

⊙ **Praying the Word**

Make me the kind of friend who draws others closer to You and challenges them to be more like Jesus by my example.

❀ **Prayer Prompt**

Bless my friends and their families. Show me ways to touch their lives with a word, favor, hug, or prayer. Bring younger women into my life that I can disciple and mentors from whom I can learn.

Reaching Beyond

☕ **Prayer Focus**–Supreme Court

📖 **Scripture Inspiration**

You shall not show partiality in judgment; . . . you shall not be afraid in any man's presence, for the judgment is God's.
(Deuteronomy 1:17 NKJV)

⊙ **Praying the Word**

Enable the justices of the Supreme Court to judge without prejudice and to fear only You.

❀ **Prayer Prompt**

I lift up all members of the court systems and ask You to guide them with wisdom and a clear conscience.

☕ Prayer Focus _____

📖 Scripture Inspiration

_____
_____

☉ Praying the Word

_____
_____

❀ Prayer Prompt

_____
_____
_____

☕ Prayer Focus _____

📖 Scripture Inspiration

_____
_____

☉ Praying the Word

_____
_____

❀ Prayer Prompt

_____
_____
_____

61

Day 7

Praise

☕ **Prayer Focus**—Love

📖 **Scripture Inspiration**

So we have come to know and to believe the love that God has for us. God is love, and whoever abides in love abides in God, and God abides in him. (1 John 4:16 ESV)

⊚ **Praying the Word**

God, I believe the love that You have for me; help me to come to know it in greater measure every day. You are love. Enable me to rest and wait so completely in Your love that I do not look to anything or anyone else to satisfy me. I want to be found wholly in You and You holy in me.

🌸 **Prayer Prompt**

I praise You, O God of Love. It is because of Your love for us that You gave the gift of Love. Your love never changes; it is the same yesterday, today, and forever. Thank You that there is nothing I can do to make You love me any less and nothing I can do to make You love me any more. Love begins and ends in You.

Prayer Focus _____

Scripture Inspiration

_____

_____

_____

_____

Praying the Word

_____

_____

_____

_____

_____

Prayer Prompt

_____

_____

_____

_____

_____

_____

_____

_____

_____

_____

Day 7
Self

Prayer Focus—Prayer Life

Scripture Inspiration

Do not be anxious about anything, but in everything by prayer and supplication with thanksgiving let your requests be made known to God. (Philippians 4:6 ESV)

Praying the Word

Dear God, I bring to You all of my concerns and needs. I thank You that You hear me and that You will answer me according to Your perfect will. Now that my desires are in Your hands, I won't worry about a thing.

Prayer Prompt

It is impossible to have a relationship without communication. My deepest desire is to know You as I am known by You. Draw me closer and closer to You through intimate conversation. Help me to remember that You desire relationship with me above anything I could ever do for You.

🍵 Prayer Focus _____

📖 Scripture Inspiration

_____
_____
_____
_____

☯ Praying the Word

_____
_____
_____
_____
_____

🌼 Prayer Prompt

_____
_____
_____
_____
_____
_____
_____
_____
_____

Day 7
Husband

Prayer Focus—Personal Walk

Scripture Inspiration

Walk in a manner worthy of the calling to which you have been called, with all humility and gentleness, with patience, bearing with one another in love. (Ephesians 4:1–2 ESV)

Praying the Word

Wherever my husband goes and whatever he does, may he remember that he is a living testimony for You. Remind him that by Your mercy, You have forgiven his sins so that he will desire to walk in humility and gentleness; with patience; being quick to understand, forgive, and love everyone he encounters.

Prayer Prompt

I pray that everything my husband thinks, says, and does will glorify You. Enable him to follow through on the heart commitment he has made to You. Encourage him to be quick to confess and repent when he strays from Your path. Give him a longing for integrity in the inner man that manifests itself in a holy walk before others.

🍵 Prayer Focus _____

📖 Scripture Inspiration

_____

_____

_____

_____

🌀 Praying the Word

_____

_____

_____

_____

_____

🌸 Prayer Prompt

_____

_____

_____

_____

_____

_____

_____

_____

_____

Day 7
Children

☕ **Prayer Focus**—Purity

📖 **Scripture Inspiration**

For this is the will of God, your sanctification: that you abstain from sexual immorality; that each one of you know how to control his own body in holiness and honor, not in the passion of lust. (1 Thessalonians 4:3–5 ESV)

☉ **Praying the Word**

Dear God, I pray that my children will walk in Your will, with lives dedicated to Your holy ways. Give them the power to honor their bodies, keep themselves sexually pure, and the ability to control the lusts of the flesh.

🌸 **Prayer Prompt**

Dear Lord, it takes supernatural power for children to remain sexually pure until marriage in today's world. So that is what I'm praying for on behalf of my children. Help them to remain in holiness and to resist the temptation to see how close to the edge they can go without falling. Remind them to use the sword of the Spirit as they hide Your word in their hearts and keep their thoughts pure as the first line of defense.

Prayer Focus_____

Scripture Inspiration

_____

_____

_____

_____

Praying the Word

_____

_____

_____

_____

_____

Prayer Prompt

_____

_____

_____

_____

_____

_____

_____

_____

_____

Day 7

Personal Influences

☕ **Prayer Focus**–Extended Family

📖 **Scripture Inspiration**

And they said, "Believe in the Lord Jesus, and you will be saved, you and your household." (Acts 16:31 ESV)

🔄 **Praying the Word**

I believe You, Jesus, as my Lord and Savior. Use me to reach every member of my family.

❀ **Prayer Prompt**

Thank You for my family. I lift up my grandparents, parents, sisters, brothers, aunts, uncles, cousins, nieces, nephews—every relative in my family—and ask that You draw them close to You. Bless them and keep them until the day of Your return.

Reaching Beyond

☕ **Prayer Focus**–Public Schools

📖 **Scripture Inspiration**

Give instruction to a wise man, and he will be still wiser; teach a righteous man, and he will increase in learning.
(Proverbs 9:9 ESV)

🔄 **Praying the Word**

Make our children wise and righteous so they will love learning and grow in understanding and knowledge.

❀ **Prayer Prompt**

Raise up godly teachers to penetrate our schools to instruct the next generation in wisdom and righteousness.

Prayer Focus _____

Scripture Inspiration

_____

_____

Praying the Word

_____

_____

Prayer Prompt

_____

_____

_____

Prayer Focus _____

Scripture Inspiration

_____

_____

Praying the Word

_____

_____

Prayer Prompt

_____

_____

_____

Day 8

Praise

Prayer Focus—Calvary

Scripture Inspiration

But God forbid that I should boast except in the cross of our Lord Jesus Christ, by whom the world has been crucified to me, and I to the world. (Galatians 6:14 NKJV)

Praying the Word

Dear God, don't let me even think of taking credit for anything that is good in me. If there be any good, it is only by the grace of my Lord Jesus Christ and the power in His blood that was shed for my sins on the cross. The world no longer has power over me. I choose to die to anything the world has to offer.

Prayer Prompt

Worthy is the Lamb who was slain to receive power and riches and wisdom and strength and honor and glory and blessing! My life began here on earth when Your life ended here on earth. Thank You for walking that painful, humiliating, unfair road to Calvary and for willingly suffering on the cross so that I might experience the abundant life You have given me.

🍵 Prayer Focus _____

📖 Scripture Inspiration

_____

_____

_____

_____

🌀 Praying the Word

_____

_____

_____

_____

_____

_____

🌸 Prayer Prompt

_____

_____

_____

_____

_____

_____

_____

_____

_____

_____

Day 8

Self

📖 Scripture Inspiration

Open my eyes, that I may see wondrous things from Your Law. (Psalm 119:18 NKJV)

☉ Praying the Word

Reveal to me the secret treasures that are hidden in Your Word, O Lord.

🌸 Prayer Prompt

I love Your law! Feed my soul as I feast on Your Word. Give me a fresh hunger to devour the Scriptures so that I am not satisfied unless I have been filled with Your truth every day. As I read, hide Your Word in my heart that I might not sin against You.

☕ Prayer Focus _____

📖 Scripture Inspiration

_____
_____
_____
_____

☯ Praying the Word

_____
_____
_____
_____
_____

❀ Prayer Prompt

_____
_____
_____
_____
_____
_____
_____
_____
_____

Day 8
Husband

Prayer Focus—Sexuality

Scripture Inspiration

Let your fountain be blessed, and rejoice with the wife of your youth. As a loving deer and a graceful doe, let her breasts satisfy you at all times; and always be enraptured with her love. (Proverbs 5:18–19 NKJV)

Praying the Word

Dear Creator, may the very life-giving source of my husband be blessed. Give us fresh enjoyment of each other and intimacy that reminds us of our first times when our love-making was full of wonder and excitement. May I be beautiful and vulnerable in my husband's eyes, and allow me to please him so completely that he is wholly satisfied with my love.

Prayer Prompt

Fortify my husband in the inner man that he might have the supernatural power to fight the lusts of the world that bombard him every day. Where there has been any history of brokenness or sin in the area of his sexuality, restore him to purity and wholeness. Bless our times of intimacy so that we become so completely one that neither the enemy nor the world nor man or woman can come between us.

Prayer Focus_____

Scripture Inspiration

_____

_____

_____

_____

Praying the Word

_____

_____

_____

_____

_____

_____

Prayer Prompt

_____

_____

_____

_____

_____

_____

_____

_____

_____

_____

Day 8

Children

📖 Scripture Inspiration

If you live according to the flesh you will die; but if by the Spirit you put to death the deeds of the body, you will live. (Romans 8:13 ESV)

☉ Praying the Word

Fill my children with Your Holy Spirit so they will have the discipline to crucify the flesh and, subsequently, be raised to new life.

❀ Prayer Prompt

Dear heavenly Father, grow the fruit of the spirit: love, joy, peace, patience, kindness, goodness, faithfulness, gentleness, and especially, self-control in my children. Help them to walk in the Spirit, and enable them to control their tempers, tongues, passions, and behavior. Remind them to call on You for strength when their flesh is weak.

Prayer Focus _____

Scripture Inspiration

_____

_____

_____

_____

Praying the Word

_____

_____

_____

_____

_____

Prayer Prompt

_____

_____

_____

_____

_____

_____

_____

_____

_____

_____

Day 8

Personal Influences

☕ **Prayer Focus**–Teachers

📖 **Scripture Inspiration**

A wise teacher's words spur students to action and emphasize important truths. (Ecclesiastes 12:11 NLT)

🔵 **Praying the Word**

Fill my children's teachers with Your creativity so they can engender excitement about learning and have the ability to express concepts with clarity.

🌸 **Prayer Prompt**

Thank You for those You have chosen to teach my children. Give them compassionate understanding, love for their job, strength for the task, and wisdom. Show me ways to support them as they fulfill the high calling of influencing so many young lives.

Reaching Beyond

☕ **Prayer Focus**–The Media

📖 **Scripture Inspiration**

See to it that no one takes you captive by philosophy and empty deceit . . . and not according to Christ. (Colossians 2:8 ESV)

🔵 **Praying the Word**

Deliver us from the spirit of this age, and set us apart from the ungodly influences of the prince of the air.

🌸 **Prayer Prompt**

Appoint godly men and women who will raise a standard of righteousness in the influential media.

Prayer Focus _____

Scripture Inspiration

_____

_____

Praying the Word

_____

_____

Prayer Prompt

_____

_____

_____

Prayer Focus _____

Scripture Inspiration

_____

_____

Praying the Word

_____

_____

Prayer Prompt

_____

_____

_____

Day 9

Praise

☕ **Prayer Focus**—Deliverer

📖 **Scripture Inspiration**

But I am poor and needy; yet the Lord thinks upon me. You are my help and my deliverer; do not delay, O my God. (Psalm 40:17 NKJV)

⊙ **Praying the Word**

I am small in worth, and yet, the Lord God Almighty thinks about me! O God, hurry up; help me and deliver me. I need You.

🌸 **Prayer Prompt**

O Jehovah, my rock, my fortress, and my deliverer! When I feel weak, You are my strength. I can't save myself, but You promise to rescue me. I feel the enemy closing in all around me, and I don't have the power to fight him anymore. All I need to do is speak the mighty name of Jesus and trust You to unleash Your authority on my behalf. Thank You for being my deliverer.

🍵 Prayer Focus _____

📖 Scripture Inspiration

_____
_____
_____
_____

⊚ Praying the Word

_____
_____
_____
_____
_____

🌼 Prayer Prompt

_____
_____
_____
_____
_____
_____
_____
_____
_____

Day 9

Self

☕ **Prayer Focus**—Confession and Repentance

📖 **Scripture Inspiration**

If we confess our sins, he is faithful and just to forgive us our sins and to cleanse us from all unrighteousness. For godly grief produces a repentance that leads to salvation without regret. (1 John 1:9; 2 Corinthians 7:10 ESV)

☉ **Praying the Word**

I want to bring my sin into the light because I am assured that You will forgive me and cleanse me completely. I am sincerely sorry for choosing my way over Yours. Help me to return to life in You.

✤ **Prayer Prompt**

I don't want to keep any sinful thought or deed hidden anymore. I confess my sin to You now, and I refuse to make any excuses for my choices. Please forgive me for turning from Your way. I want to follow You again. Change me from within by the power of the risen Lord.

☕ Prayer Focus_____

📖 Scripture Inspiration

_____
_____
_____
_____

🌀 Praying the Word

_____
_____
_____
_____
_____
_____

🌸 Prayer Prompt

_____
_____
_____
_____
_____
_____
_____
_____
_____

Day 9
Husband

☕ **Prayer Focus**—Health

📖 **Scripture Inspiration**

I will restore health to you, and your wounds I will heal.
(Jeremiah 30:17 ESV)

⊚ **Praying the Word**

Thank You for Your promise, Lord, that You will heal my
husband and give him good health.

❀ **Prayer Prompt**

Standing on Your Word, I pray for health, strength, and a
long life for my husband. If there is any hidden infirmity,
You can see it, so heal that too. I ask for a special touch of
healing on his heart, both physically and emotionally. Take
sickness away from the midst of him, and keep disease
from him. Thank You that he will fulfill all the number of
days You have planned for him.

🍵 Prayer Focus _____

📖 Scripture Inspiration

_____

_____

_____

_____

🌀 Praying the Word

_____

_____

_____

_____

_____

🌸 Prayer Prompt

_____

_____

_____

_____

_____

_____

_____

_____

_____

_____

87

Day 9
Children

Scripture Inspiration

All your children shall be taught by the Lord, and great shall be the peace of your children. (Isaiah 54:13 ESV)

Praying the Word

Teach my children, Lord, and thank You for the peace they will enjoy by following Your instruction.

Prayer Prompt

First of all, I pray that my children will learn from You and seek Your wisdom, Lord. Beyond that I ask that You will grant my children a love for learning. Give them the ability to understand the things they are being taught and remember them even beyond the tests. Teach them to organize their assignments and their time wisely. Help them to be respectful of those in authority and to find favor with their teachers and classmates.

Prayer Focus _____

Scripture Inspiration

_____

_____

_____

_____

Praying the Word

_____

_____

_____

_____

_____

_____

Prayer Prompt

_____

_____

_____

_____

_____

_____

_____

_____

_____

_____

Day 9
Personal Influences

Prayer Focus–In-laws

Scripture Inspiration
In you all the families of the earth shall be blessed.
(Genesis 12:3 ESV)

Praying the Word
Dear God, please use me to bless every member of my husband's family.

Prayer Prompt
I am so grateful for the husband You have allowed me to marry. I understand that along with the blessing of marrying into his family came my responsibility to show love, mercy, forgiveness, hospitality, and Christ's character. Please help me to do that.

Reaching Beyond

Prayer Focus–The Military

Scripture Inspiration
The horse is made ready for the day of battle, but the victory belongs to the Lord. (Proverbs 21:31 ESV)

Praying the Word
Prepare the military strength of our nation, but remind us to put our faith in You, the Commander of the Lord's army.

Prayer Prompt
Thank You for the many men and women who serve in our nation's military. Bless them and keep them. Wrap Your arms of protection around them and their families.

☕ Prayer Focus _____

📖 Scripture Inspiration

_____

_____

☉ Praying the Word

_____

_____

❀ Prayer Prompt

_____

_____

_____

☕ Prayer Focus _____

📖 Scripture Inspiration

_____

_____

☉ Praying the Word

_____

_____

❀ Prayer Prompt

_____

_____

_____

Day 10

Praise

☕ **Prayer Focus**—Heavenly Father

📖 **Scripture Inspiration**

For the Father Himself loves you, because you have loved Me and have believed that I came from God. (John 16:27 ESV)

☺ **Praying the Word**

I am amazed that You, the Father of all, love me because I love Your Son, and I believe with all my heart that He is the Son of God and was sent by You.

🌸 **Prayer Prompt**

Dear heavenly Father, I long to curl up in Your lap like a little girl, rest in Your strong arms, and lay my head upon Your chest where I can hear Your heart beating with Your love for me, Your precious child. Thank You for the privilege of calling You "Abba." I love You, Daddy.

Prayer Focus_____

Scripture Inspiration

_____
_____
_____
_____

Praying the Word

_____
_____
_____
_____
_____

Prayer Prompt

_____
_____
_____
_____
_____
_____
_____
_____
_____

Day 10

Self

☕ **Prayer Focus**—Faith

📖**Scripture Inspiration**

Without faith it is impossible to please Him, for he who comes to God must believe that He is, and that He is a rewarder of those who diligently seek Him. (Hebrews 11:6 NASB)

☉ **Praying the Word**

I come to You, believing that You are the Almighty, Living God. I want to seek You with all my heart because I know that You are a rewarder. The greatest reward I could receive is pleasing You; give me that kind of faith.

🌼 **Prayer Prompt**

I believe; help my unbelief. I humbly ask for the gift of faith that I might believe the promises You have made to me. Help me to so trust You that I begin thanking You in advance for answers to prayers that I cannot yet see. Increase my faith so that I can receive all that You have in store for me and the others I pray for.

🍵 Prayer Focus_____

📖 Scripture Inspiration

_____
_____
_____
_____

🌀 Praying the Word

_____
_____
_____
_____
_____
_____

🦋 Prayer Prompt

_____
_____
_____
_____
_____
_____
_____
_____
_____
_____

Day 10
Husband

☕ **Prayer Focus**—Humility

📖 **Scripture Inspiration**

Let nothing be done through selfish ambition or conceit, but in lowliness of mind let each esteem others better than himself. (Philippians 2:3 NKJV)

☺ **Praying the Word**

Help my husband to serve others and even put them before himself. Keep him from selfishness or his own agenda or thinking more of himself than he should. Remind him of Your mercy toward him when he was yet a sinner.

❀ **Prayer Prompt**

Open my husband's eyes to glimpse as much of Your glory as he can handle. May seeing You cause a natural humility and ongoing waves of worship. Remind him that anything that is praiseworthy in him comes from Your good hand. Teach him to enjoy walking in Your shadow.

☕ Prayer Focus _____

📖 Scripture Inspiration

_____
_____
_____
_____

⊙ Praying the Word

_____
_____
_____
_____
_____

❀ Prayer Prompt

_____
_____
_____
_____
_____
_____
_____
_____
_____

Day 10

Children

📖 Scripture Inspiration

I will put My laws into their minds, and write them on their hearts, and I will be their God, and they shall be my people. (Hebrews 8:10 ESV)

☉ Praying the Word

Almighty God, I ask You to put Your laws in my children's minds and write them on their hearts. I pray they will make You their God and will be Your people.

❀ Prayer Prompt

Father, my goal as a parent is that ultimately my children will love You and obey You from their hearts. As I train them from the outside-in, I ask You to shape and mold their hearts from the inside-out. I come against any legalism or obedience that is only for show. I pray that out of their hearts will flow rivers of living water. Thank You.

🍵 Prayer Focus_____

📖 Scripture Inspiration

_____
_____
_____
_____

🌀 Praying the Word

_____
_____
_____
_____
_____
_____

🌸 Prayer Prompt

_____
_____
_____
_____
_____
_____
_____
_____
_____

Day 10

Personal Influences

☕ **Prayer Focus**–Kids' Friends

📖 **Scripture Inspiration**
Do not be deceived: "Bad company ruins good morals."
(1 Corinthians 15:33 ESV)

🕓 **Praying the Word**
Encourage each of my children's friends to make right choices
so they can build each other up in their walk with You.

🌸 **Prayer Prompt**
Thank You for my children's friends. Keep each one safe, and
help them grow in wisdom, stature, and in favor with You and
man. Enable my children to be a good influence and a strong witness of the wisdom in following You.

Reaching Beyond

☕ **Prayer Focus**–The House and Senate

📖 **Scripture Inspiration**
*You will live under a government that is just and fair. Your ene-
mies will stay far away; you will live in peace. Terror will not
come near.* (Isaiah 54:14 NLT)

🕓 **Praying the Word**
Make our government just and fair. Keep our enemies far away,
hold back any threat of terrorism, and give us peace.

🌸 **Prayer Prompt**
Purge all politics from government, and instead, may we as a
nation be driven by what is right and good in Your sight.

☕ Prayer Focus_____

📖 Scripture Inspiration

_____

_____

◎ Praying the Word

_____

_____

❀ Prayer Prompt

_____

_____

_____

☕ Prayer Focus_____

📖 Scripture Inspiration

_____

_____

◎ Praying the Word

_____

_____

❀ Prayer Prompt

_____

_____

_____

Day 11

Praise

📖 Scripture Inspiration

No longer do I call you servants, for the servant does not know what his master is doing; but I have called you friends, for all that I have heard from my Father I have made known to you. (John 15:15 ESV)

☉ Praying the Word

I cannot believe that the God of the universe calls me friend. Even if You, Jesus, no longer call me servant, I long to be Your servant. Help me to know You, Master, and Your purposes. Open my ears to hear everything You reveal to me from Your Father.

🌸 Prayer Prompt

It is beyond my imagination that You would want me as a friend, but I will accept Your mercy and gratefully welcome Your friendship. Thank You for walking beside me through the dailyness of my days. Sweet Jesus, You are that friend who sticks closer than a brother. I'm so happy to know that nothing can separate me from Your love.

Prayer Focus _____

Scripture Inspiration

_____

_____

_____

_____

Praying the Word

_____

_____

_____

_____

_____

_____

Prayer Prompt

_____

_____

_____

_____

_____

_____

_____

_____

_____

Day 11

Self

Scripture Inspiration

Having gifts that differ according to the grace given to us, let us use them. (Romans 12:6 ESV)

Praying the Word

Thank You for the specific gifts that You have given me by Your grace. Help me to use them for Your glory.

Prayer Prompt

Anoint me to minister in ways and to those You have called me to serve. Keep me from coveting someone else's gifts, talents, or calling. Reveal to me the plans You have to use my gifts so that I may lay them at Your feet and be used by You according to Your will. May You be glorified through me.

🍵 Prayer Focus _____

📖 Scripture Inspiration

_____
_____
_____
_____

☉ Praying the Word

_____
_____
_____
_____
_____
_____

🌸 Prayer Prompt

_____
_____
_____
_____
_____
_____
_____
_____
_____

Day 11
Husband

☕ **Prayer Focus**—Protection

📖 **Scripture Inspiration**

You have hedged me behind and before, and laid Your hand upon me. (Psalm 139:5 NKJV)

☉ **Praying the Word**

What peace to know that You have surrounded my husband with Your protection and that every aspect of his life is completely in Your trustworthy hand.

🦋 **Prayer Prompt**

Thank You, Father, for protecting my husband, our household, and all that he has on every side. Put angels all around him to keep him from any accidents or injuries. Stand guard over his reputation or any traps the evil one may have set for him. I will rest today knowing that no weapon formed against him will prosper. He is safe in Your hands.

🍵 Prayer Focus _____

📖 Scripture Inspiration

_____

_____

_____

_____

🌀 Praying the Word

_____

_____

_____

_____

_____

🌸 Prayer Prompt

_____

_____

_____

_____

_____

_____

_____

_____

_____

Day 11
Children

☕ **Prayer Focus**—Thoughts

📖 **Scripture Inspiration**

Whatever is true, whatever is honorable, whatever is just, whatever is pure, whatever is lovely, whatever is commendable, if there is any excellence, if there is anything worthy of praise, think about these things. (Philippians 4:8 ESV)

☉ **Praying the Word**

Sweet Lord, direct my children's thoughts to only dwell on things that are true, honorable, just, pure, lovely, commendable, excellent, and worthy of praise.

🌸 **Prayer Prompt**

Heavenly Father, I can't read my children's minds, but You can. Would You please pay close attention to the things they are thinking and redirect their thoughts when they aren't pleasing to You? If they begin stuffing their feelings, harboring fear, sinking into depression, or believing lies, please bring these thoughts out into the open so we can bring them before Your healing Light of Truth. Fill their thoughts with Your love and life.

Prayer Focus_____

Scripture Inspiration

_____

_____

_____

_____

Praying the Word

_____

_____

_____

_____

_____

_____

Prayer Prompt

_____

_____

_____

_____

_____

_____

_____

_____

_____

_____

Day 11

Personal Influences

☕ **Prayer Focus**–Kids' Friends' Parents

📖 **Scripture Inspiration**

Children, obey your parents in everything, for this pleases the Lord. (Colossians 3:20 ESV)

🔾 **Praying the Word**

Fortify the parents of my children's friends to require obedience in everything so they may know and enjoy Your pleasure.

🌸 **Prayer Prompt**

Lord, I know friends greatly influence my children. Please strengthen the homes of my children's friends. Because of a sure foundation at home, may my children and their friends find support from each other to stand firm in the midst of peer pressure.

Reaching Beyond

☕ **Prayer Focus**–Enemies

📖 **Scripture Inspiration**

I say to you, "Love your enemies and pray for those who persecute you." (Matthew 5:43 ESV)

🔾 **Praying the Word**

We obey Your commands as we pray for our enemies, and we ask You to reveal how we can show them Your love.

🌸 **Prayer Prompt**

Lord, I lift up those who have personally hurt me. I will to forgive them, and I give up my rights and requirements of restitution. I ask You to bless them.

☕ Prayer Focus _____

📖 Scripture Inspiration

_____
_____

⊙ Praying the Word

_____
_____

❀ Prayer Prompt

_____
_____
_____

☕ Prayer Focus _____

📖 Scripture Inspiration

_____
_____

⊙ Praying the Word

_____
_____

❀ Prayer Prompt

_____
_____
_____

Day 12

Praise

☕ **Prayer Focus**—Counselor

📖 **Scripture Inspiration**

And His name shall be called Wonderful Counselor, Mighty God, Everlasting Father, Prince of Peace. (Isaiah 9:6 ESV)

⊙ **Praying the Word**

Help me to know You, Lord, as the Wonderful Counselor, Mighty God, the Everlasting Father, and the Prince of Peace.

🦋 **Prayer Prompt**

The wisdom of the Creator of the galaxies has offered His counsel to me. I humbly bow before You and thank You for Your guidance. May I have a teachable spirit that I might honor every truth that You so graciously reveal to me. It is my fervent desire to seek Your will in every area of my life. I submit to Your counsel and worship You as Wonderful Counselor.

Prayer Focus _____

Scripture Inspiration

_____
_____
_____
_____

Praying the Word

_____
_____
_____
_____
_____

Prayer Prompt

_____
_____
_____
_____
_____
_____
_____
_____
_____
_____

Day 12
Self

☕ **Prayer Focus**—My Offspring

📖 **Scripture Inspiration**

In your offspring shall all the nations of the earth be blessed, because you have obeyed my voice. (Genesis 22:18 ESV)

🔿 **Praying the Word**

Father God, help me to withhold nothing from You but to walk in complete trust and obedience. Thank You for the promise that You will bless the nations of the earth through my offspring.

🌸 **Prayer Prompt**

I know how earnestly I pray for my children because I love them so desperately. I can only imagine that I will certainly feel at least that strong of emotion and concern for my grandchildren. Because I believe that my love will increase exponentially with each generation, I pray in advance for salvation and abundant life for every child that will ultimately proceed from me until the return of Christ Jesus.

🍵 Prayer Focus _____

📖 Scripture Inspiration

_____

_____

_____

_____

🌀 Praying the Word

_____

_____

_____

_____

_____

🌸 Prayer Prompt

_____

_____

_____

_____

_____

_____

_____

_____

_____

_____

Day 12
Husband

☕ **Prayer Focus**—Integrity

📖 **Scripture Inspiration**

He who walks with integrity walks securely. (Proverbs 10:9 NKJV)

◎ **Praying the Word**

May my husband walk with a heart that is clean before You so that he has nothing to be afraid of.

❀ **Prayer Prompt**

Prompt my husband to invite You into the secret places of his heart. Search his heart, and illuminate anything that is hiding in the shadows. May he so enjoy walking in the light as You are in the light that he would not tolerate even a hint of darkness. May he live his life before an audience of One.

Prayer Focus _____

Scripture Inspiration

_____
_____
_____
_____

Praying the Word

_____
_____
_____
_____
_____
_____

Prayer Prompt

_____
_____
_____
_____
_____
_____
_____
_____
_____
_____

Day 12
Children

📖 **Scripture Inspiration**

*Let the words of my mouth and the meditation of my heart
be acceptable in Your sight, O Lord, my strength and my
redeemer.* (Psalm 19:14 NKJV)

⊚ **Praying the Word**

O Lord, redeem my children and be their strength. As You
keep Your eyes upon them, let everything they think and
say be acceptable to You.

🌸 **Prayer Prompt**

Dear God, You are their Father, so help them to speak truth
and not lies. Teach them to bridle their tongues, and
strengthen their resolve not to fall into bad habits of coarse
jesting, inappropriate humor, or profanity of any kind. May
they cringe at the thought of hurting someone with their
words. Instead, may they know the joy of speaking just the
right word at the right time.

🍵 Prayer Focus _____

📖 Scripture Inspiration

_____

_____

_____

_____

🌀 Praying the Word

_____

_____

_____

_____

_____

🌸 Prayer Prompt

_____

_____

_____

_____

_____

_____

_____

_____

_____

Day 12
Personal Influences

☕ **Prayer Focus**–Pets

📖 **Scripture Inspiration**
A righteous man regards the life of his animal.
(Proverbs 12:10 NKJV)

☉ **Praying the Word**
Lord, help our family to learn responsibility and grow in righteousness as we take good care of our pets.

🦋 **Prayer Prompt**
Thank You for the joy and unconditional love our pets give us. Help us give them the time and attention they need. Teach my children as they care for them, and help them make wonderful childhood memories. Please keep our pets safe and healthy.

Reaching Beyond

☕ **Prayer Focus**–Missionaries

📖 **Scripture Inspiration**
Pray earnestly to the Lord of the harvest to send out laborers into his harvest. (Matthew 9:37–38 ESV)

☉ **Praying the Word**
Raise up men and women who feel Your call on their lives to go into the world to preach the gospel of Jesus Christ.

🦋 **Prayer Prompt**
Comfort and strengthen all who are already laboring throughout the earth. Encourage their hearts, and pour out fresh anointing on them.

🍵 Prayer Focus _____

📖 Scripture Inspiration

_____

_____

⊙ Praying the Word

_____

_____

🌸 Prayer Prompt

_____

_____

_____

🍵 Prayer Focus _____

📖 Scripture Inspiration

_____

_____

⊙ Praying the Word

_____

_____

🌸 Prayer Prompt

_____

_____

_____

Day 13

Praise

☕ **Prayer Focus**—Healer

📖 **Scripture Inspiration**

And when Jesus went out He saw a great multitude; and He was moved with compassion for them, and healed their sick. (Matthew 14:14 NKJV)

☉ **Praying the Word**

Jesus, I know that even amidst the multitude, You see me. I believe that my needs touch Your heart and that You can heal me.

❀ **Prayer Prompt**

Jesus, You are the same yesterday, today, and forever. I am so grateful that You are still in the miracle-working business. I believe that by Your stripes I am healed, and I worship You as the Resurrection and the Life. O Keeper of the keys of death, I exalt You.

Prayer Focus _____

Scripture Inspiration

_____
_____
_____
_____

Praying the Word

_____
_____
_____
_____
_____
_____

Prayer Prompt

_____
_____
_____
_____
_____
_____
_____
_____
_____
_____

Day 13

Self

☕ **Prayer Focus**—Health

📖 **Scripture Inspiration**

Beloved, I pray that all may go well with you and that you may be in good health, as it goes well with your soul.
(3 John 2 ESV)

☉ **Praying the Word**

I receive the apostle John's prayers for myself that all may go well with me and that I may be healthy in body and soul.

❀ **Prayer Prompt**

Jesus, as You walked the earth, You healed the sick and the brokenhearted. You also said if I asked, I would receive. So I'm asking that You would give me good health. Keep me from sickness and disease of the body, soul, or mind. Make me strong and healthy so that I can serve You diligently all the days of my life. Should You choose in Your wisdom and mercy to allow me to suffer, let it bring You glory.

Prayer Focus _____

Scripture Inspiration

_____

_____

_____

_____

Praying the Word

_____

_____

_____

_____

_____

Prayer Prompt

_____

_____

_____

_____

_____

_____

_____

_____

_____

Day 13

Husband

☕ **Prayer Focus**—Thought Life

📖 **Scripture Inspiration**

You keep him in perfect peace whose mind is stayed on you, because he trusts in you. (Isaiah 26:3 ESV)

☺ **Praying the Word**

Help my husband to keep his thoughts so focused on You and Your trustworthiness that he rests completely in Your plan for his life.

🌸 **Prayer Prompt**

Train my husband to think about You, Your Word, and Your ways when he is tempted by the enemy in his thought life. Cleanse him from any impure, anxious, or deceiving thoughts, and strengthen him to hold fast to the Truth. Make him diligent to keep the door to his heart guarded as he takes every thought captive to the obedience of Christ.

Prayer Focus_____

Scripture Inspiration

_____
_____
_____
_____

Praying the Word

_____
_____
_____
_____
_____

Prayer Prompt

_____
_____
_____
_____
_____
_____
_____
_____
_____

Day 13
Children

☕ **Prayer Focus**—Protection

📖 **Scripture Inspiration**

Pour out your heart like water before the face of the Lord. Lift your hands toward Him for the life of your young children. (Lamentations 2:19 NKJV)

☉ **Praying the Word**

I come before You, Lord, and pour out my heart to You. I surrender my children to You and ask that You would keep and protect them all the days of their lives.

🌸 **Prayer Prompt**

Thankfully, I know that You love my dear children even more than I do. With that in mind, I hand them over to You. I am confident that You have given Your angels charge over my children and they will keep them in all their ways. Help me not to fear but to rest in Your ability to protect my children and to trust that the enemy will not be allowed to touch my children without Your permission. They are safe with You.

Prayer Focus_____

Scripture Inspiration

_____
_____
_____
_____

Praying the Word

_____
_____
_____
_____
_____

Prayer Prompt

_____
_____
_____
_____
_____
_____
_____
_____
_____
_____

Day 13
Personal Influences

☕ **Prayer Focus**–Boss

📖 **Scripture Inspiration**

If the master returns and finds that the servant has done a good job, there will be a reward. (Matthew 24:46 NLT)

🕑 **Praying the Word**

Lord, I pray that my husband's (and/or my) boss would be happy with the job being done, recognize integrity and hard work, and reward appropriately.

🦋 **Prayer Prompt**

Please bless my husband's (and/or my) boss. Give him grace to manage and wisdom to make good decisions. May his personal life and his business endeavors prosper. If he doesn't know You, open his eyes through my husband (and/or me.)

Reaching Beyond

☕ **Prayer Focus**–The Economy

📖 **Scripture Inspiration**

Your God will bless you . . . and you shall lend to many nations, but you shall not borrow. (Deuteronomy 16:6 ESV)

🕑 **Praying the Word**

We stand on Your Word, believing that we are called to be a ruling nation that is rich in generosity and not in debt.

🦋 **Prayer Prompt**

May we as a nation spend wisely and with integrity. Create jobs so that everyone can provide for their own families. In mercy bless us, Lord.

🍵 Prayer Focus _____

📖 Scripture Inspiration

_____

_____

⚙ Praying the Word

_____

_____

✿ Prayer Prompt

_____

_____

_____

🍵 Prayer Focus _____

📖 Scripture Inspiration

_____

_____

⚙ Praying the Word

_____

_____

✿ Prayer Prompt

_____

_____

_____

Day 14

Praise

☕ **Prayer Focus**—Provider

📖 **Scripture Inspiration**

If you then, being evil, know how to give good gifts to your children, how much more will your Father who is in heaven give good things to those who ask Him. (Matthew 7:11 NKJV)

⊙ **Praying the Word**

Father, I know even I, as a sinful parent, love to give good gifts to my children. You, who own the storehouses of heaven, love to give good things to us as Your children even more! You are just waiting for us to ask. So, here's me asking.

❀ **Prayer Prompt**

I will not worry about tomorrow because I know that You already have a plan to supply all of my needs according to Your riches in glory by Christ Jesus. Therefore, I praise You now for that which I cannot see, and by faith I will thank You in advance because I know You are trustworthy. Thank You for providing for my every need (and more wants than I should have). I am grateful to You, my generous Gift Giver.

Prayer Focus_____

Scripture Inspiration

_____
_____
_____
_____

Praying the Word

_____
_____
_____
_____
_____

Prayer Prompt

_____
_____
_____
_____
_____
_____
_____
_____
_____
_____

133

Day 14

Self

☕ **Prayer Focus**—Relationships

📖 **Scripture Inspiration**

Pursue peace with all people, and holiness, without which no one will see the Lord. (Hebrews 12:14 NKJV)

◎ **Praying the Word**

I pray that people will see You, Lord, through me as I strive to walk in holiness by Your Spirit working in me. Help me to be a peacemaker in all of my relationships.

❀ **Prayer Prompt**

Lord, would You please use me to touch the people in my life with Your love and life? I pray for peaceful relationships without strife or confusion. Give me the kind of "iron sharpens iron," "speak the truth in love," and "fellowship of the Spirit" friendships with other women.

Prayer Focus_____

Scripture Inspiration

_____
_____
_____
_____

Praying the Word

_____
_____
_____
_____
_____
_____

Prayer Prompt

_____
_____
_____
_____
_____
_____
_____
_____
_____
_____

Day 14
Husband

☕ **Prayer Focus**—Words

📖 **Scripture Inspiration**

Let no corrupting talk come out of your mouths, but only such as is good for building up, as fits the occasion, that it may give grace to those who hear. (Ephesians 4:29 ESV)

◎ **Praying the Word**

Lord, I pray that every word my husband speaks would encourage, be appropriate, be honest, and would bless those around him.

🌸 **Prayer Prompt**

Thank You for the gift of communication. Reveal to my husband the power he possesses to create life with his words. Help him understand how much I love to hear what he has to say and how his words affect me and the children. Teach him to guard his tongue from coarse talk, lies, criticism, broken promises, and words spoken in anger. May his words flow from a heart that loves Your Word.

Prayer Focus _____

Scripture Inspiration

_____

_____

_____

_____

Praying the Word

_____

_____

_____

_____

_____

Prayer Prompt

_____

_____

_____

_____

_____

_____

_____

_____

_____

Day 14
Children

📖 **Scripture Inspiration**

Bless the Lord, O my soul, and forget not all his benefits,
who forgives all your iniquity and heals all your diseases.
(Psalm 103:2–3 ESV)

☉ Praying the Word

I bless You, Lord, with everything that's within me. Help
my children never to forget all Your blessings toward them,
especially the forgiveness of their sins. Thank You for the
added blessing of Your power to heal them. I claim that
now for my children.

❀ Prayer Prompt

Father, I ask You to give my children good health.
Strengthen their immune systems. Keep them from accidents. Any diseases that might try to rear their ugly heads,
cover now with Your healing hand. Great Physician, should
You decide to heal them through the blessing of medicine,
lead us to the doctors You have chosen for them and anoint
their hands with the power of Your touch.

Prayer Focus _____

Scripture Inspiration

_____
_____
_____
_____

Praying the Word

_____
_____
_____
_____
_____

Prayer Prompt

_____
_____
_____
_____
_____
_____
_____
_____
_____

Day 14

Personal Influences

☕ **Prayer Focus**–Coworkers

📖 **Scripture Inspiration**

You yourself must be an example to them by doing good deeds of every kind. Let everything you do reflect the integrity and seriousness of your teaching. (Titus 2:7 NLT)

🕙 **Praying the Word**

Allow my husband (and/or me) to be a good example to his/my coworkers. Let them see the character of Jesus in everything we do.

🌸 **Prayer Prompt**

Use my husband (and/or me) to draw coworkers to You. May they watch us and desire to know You personally. Bless their families, and give them fresh joy in their jobs. May peace reign throughout the company.

Reaching Beyond

☕ **Prayer Focus**–Jerusalem

📖 **Scripture Inspiration**

Pray for the peace of Jerusalem: "May they prosper who love you." (Psalm 122:6 NKJV)

🕙 **Praying the Word**

Dear God, we love Jerusalem, and we pray for the peace of Your holy city.

🌸 **Prayer Prompt**

Father, we ask for peace to reign in the Middle East and especially throughout Israel. Until Your return, hold back the killing and terrorizing of Your children.

Prayer Focus_____

Scripture Inspiration

_____
_____

Praying the Word

_____
_____

Prayer Prompt

_____
_____
_____

Prayer Focus_____

Scripture Inspiration

_____
_____

Praying the Word

_____
_____

Prayer Prompt

_____
_____
_____

Day 15

Praise

☕ **Prayer Focus**—Peace

📖 **Scripture Inspiration**

Peace I leave with you; my peace I give to you. Not as the world gives do I give to you. Let not your hearts be troubled, neither let them be afraid. (John 14:27 ESV)

☉ **Praying the Word**

Lord Jesus, before You ascended to Your Father, You promised to leave Your peace with us. You have given me peace. Not the transitory kind the world offers, but lasting peace. Help me not to be anxious or afraid.

🌸 **Prayer Prompt**

Thank You for the peace that passes understanding. I praise You for the supernatural calm that surrounds me, even in the midst of storms that rage around me. Speak "Peace, be still" to my heart when I begin to toss and turn in the tumult. You are my Prince of Peace, and I will trust in You.

☕ Prayer Focus _____

📖 Scripture Inspiration

_____
_____
_____
_____

⊙ Praying the Word

_____
_____
_____
_____
_____

❀ Prayer Prompt

_____
_____
_____
_____
_____
_____
_____
_____
_____

Day 15
Self

☕ **Prayer Focus**—Diet

📖 **Scripture Inspiration**

So, whether you eat or drink, or whatever you do, do all to the glory of God. (1 Corinthians 10:31 ESV)

☺ **Praying the Word**

May everything that I eat or drink—and anything else I do, for that matter—always be a good witness of You.

🌸 **Prayer Prompt**

I know that my body is the temple of the Holy Spirit. I desire to keep Your home strong, beautiful, and comfortable. Help me not to be as concerned about what the outside of Your house looks like as I am about the inside, where You live. Give me the self-discipline to eat foods that will keep my body well-built and long lasting.

Prayer Focus _____

Scripture Inspiration

_____

_____

_____

_____

Praying the Word

_____

_____

_____

_____

_____

Prayer Prompt

_____

_____

_____

_____

_____

_____

_____

_____

_____

_____

Day 15
Husband

📖 **Scripture Inspiration**

He must manage his own household well, with all dignity keeping his children submissive, for if someone does not know how to manage his own household, how will he care for God's church. (1 Timothy 3:4–5 ESV)

☉ **Praying the Word**

Anoint my husband to lead our family well. Because of his servant leadership, may he expect obedience from our children. Expand his influence to our church, and give him Your heart for those he leads in all arenas.

🌸 **Prayer Prompt**

Dear God, raise up my husband to be a strong commander in Your army. May he walk in Your authority wherever the sole of his foot trods. Give him a servant's heart and a leader's courage.

🍵 Prayer Focus_____

📖 Scripture Inspiration

_____

_____

_____

_____

⊙ Praying the Word

_____

_____

_____

_____

_____

🌸 Prayer Prompt

_____

_____

_____

_____

_____

_____

_____

_____

_____

Day 15

Children

☕ **Prayer Focus**—Gifts and Calling

📖 **Scripture Inspiration**
Having gifts that differ according to the grace given to us, let us use them. (Romans 12:6 ESV)

🕐 **Praying the Word**
Thank You, Lord, that You give each of us in Your body different gifts. May my children be diligent to use the gifts You have so graciously given them to glorify You.

🌼 **Prayer Prompt**
Heavenly Father, I ask You to reveal to my children at an early age the gifts You have given them and the calling and purpose for which You have created them. Keep them from looking in other directions so they don't waste time going down paths that will not ultimately be blessed or useful for Your kingdom. May they appreciate the gifts and enjoy the calling You have for them and never covet someone else's gifts or calling.

Prayer Focus _____

Scripture Inspiration

_____

_____

_____

_____

Praying the Word

_____

_____

_____

_____

_____

Prayer Prompt

_____

_____

_____

_____

_____

_____

_____

_____

_____

Day 15

Personal Influences

☕ **Prayer Focus**—Neighbors

📖 **Scripture Inspiration**

Better is a neighbor who is near than a brother who is far away.
(Proverbs 27:10 ESV)

🕲 **Praying the Word**

Thank You for the gift of close neighbors. May our neighborhood
be like a family as we reach out to serve one another.

❀ **Prayer Prompt**

May Your spirit reign over our neighborhood and Your light shine
from house to house. Place angels as guards over our homes and
families, and use my hands to touch my neighbors with Your love.

Reaching Beyond

☕ **Prayer Focus**—The Poor and Defenseless

📖 **Scripture Inspiration**

*Defend the poor and fatherless; do justice to the afflicted and
needy.* (Psalm 82:3 NKJV)

🕲 **Praying the Word**

Lord, we lift up those who are living in poverty and without
fathers. Help us to reach out to those in need.

❀ **Prayer Prompt**

Father, You see all of the world's broken hearts. Reach down with
Your tender mercy and allow each one of them to sense Your love
and plan for their lives.

☕ Prayer Focus _____

📖 Scripture Inspiration

_____

_____

☉ Praying the Word

_____

_____

❀ Prayer Prompt

_____

_____

_____

☕ Prayer Focus _____

📖 Scripture Inspiration

_____

_____

☉ Praying the Word

_____

_____

❀ Prayer Prompt

_____

_____

_____

Day 16

Praise

☕ **Prayer Focus**—Comforter

📖 **Scripture Inspiration**

And I will pray the Father, and he shall give you another Comforter, that he may be with you for ever. (John 14:16 ASV)

⊙ **Praying the Word**

Dear Father, thank You for giving me the Comforter. I know there is nothing I can go through that He will not be right beside me, even inside me.

❧ **Prayer Prompt**

Thank You for caring enough about my feelings that You specifically sent the Comforter to wrap Your arms around me when I am sad, disappointed, or afraid. I am grateful for Your presence that surrounds, consoles, and covers me.

🍵 Prayer Focus _____

📖 Scripture Inspiration

_____

_____

_____

_____

⊙ Praying the Word

_____

_____

_____

_____

_____

🌸 Prayer Prompt

_____

_____

_____

_____

_____

_____

_____

_____

_____

_____

Day 16

Self

📖 Scripture Inspiration

But I discipline my body and keep it under control.
(1 Corinthians 9:27 ESV)

⊙ Praying the Word

Give me the strength to submit my flesh to the control of
Your Spirit.

❀ Prayer Prompt

Help me to take good care of this earthen vessel through
which You have chosen to fill and demonstrate Your excellent power. Strengthen me to make daily exercise some
kind of priority so I can keep my heart and body strong.
Allow me to feel the exhilaration that comes from exercise,
and may it lift my spirits, clear my mind, and boost my
energy for the tasks You've given me.

🍵 Prayer Focus _____

📖 Scripture Inspiration

_____

_____

_____

_____

🌀 Praying the Word

_____

_____

_____

_____

_____

🌸 Prayer Prompt

_____

_____

_____

_____

_____

_____

_____

_____

_____

_____

Day 16
Husband

☕ **Prayer Focus**—Self-Control

📖 **Scripture Inspiration**

A man without self-control is like a city broken into and left without walls. (Proverbs 25:28 ESV)

☺ **Praying the Word**

Dear Lord, guard and protect my husband by strengthening him with self-control.

❀ **Prayer Prompt**

Give my husband ability to walk in the spirit and not in the flesh. Keep him from angry outbursts, lustful indulgences, foolish impulses, harmful addictions, and careless words. Show him the power in a man who has learned to call out to You in his times of weakness. When he stumbles may he be quick to repent and reach up for Your hand to stand again.

Prayer Focus_____

Scripture Inspiration

_____

_____

_____

_____

Praying the Word

_____

_____

_____

_____

_____

Prayer Prompt

_____

_____

_____

_____

_____

_____

_____

_____

_____

Day 16
Children

☕ **Prayer Focus**—Repentance

📖 **Scripture Inspiration**

He who covers his sins will not prosper, but whoever confesses and forsakes them will have mercy. (Proverbs 28:13 NKJV)

🕊 **Praying the Word**

Teach my children the wisdom and freedom in confessing their sins and the power available to walk away from them. May they trust Your mercy and not be tempted to hide their sins, which leads to destruction.

❀ **Prayer Prompt**

One of the most important things I want to ask for my children is that they know and love mercy. Reveal Your love for them so completely that they immediately confess their sin and repent because they can't stand even a moment's separation from You. May they boldly approach the throne of grace to receive strength not to sin again.

Prayer Focus _____

Scripture Inspiration

_____
_____
_____
_____

Praying the Word

_____
_____
_____
_____
_____
_____

Prayer Prompt

_____
_____
_____
_____
_____
_____
_____
_____
_____
_____

Day 16

Personal Influences

☕ **Prayer Focus**—Unsaved Friends

📖 **Scripture Inspiration**
No one can come to me unless the Father who sent me draws him.
(John 6:44 ESV)

◎ **Praying the Word**
Dear Heavenly Father, I ask You to draw _____ into
a personal relationship with Jesus by Your Holy Spirit.

❀ **Prayer Prompt**
Please bring people into my life who don't know You so that I
may have the privilege of sharing You through my life. Give me
opportunities, words, and courage to tell them about Your plan of
salvation, forgiveness, and hope for their lives.

Reaching Beyond

☕ **Prayer Focus**—Crime/Terrorism

📖 **Scripture Inspiration**
*Do not be afraid of sudden terror, nor of trouble from the wicked
when it comes; for the Lord will be your confidence.* (Proverbs
3:25–26 NKJV)

◎ **Praying the Word**
Thank You for Your protection and Your promise to keep us from
trouble and the plans of the wicked.

❀ **Prayer Prompt**
We call upon You, Almighty God, to be our defender, fortress,
and strong tower. We will run to You and be safe.

🍵 Prayer Focus_____

📖 Scripture Inspiration

_____

_____

⊙ Praying the Word

_____

_____

✿ Prayer Prompt

_____

_____

_____

🍵 Prayer Focus_____

📖 Scripture Inspiration

_____

_____

⊙ Praying the Word

_____

_____

✿ Prayer Prompt

_____

_____

_____

161

Day 17

Praise

☕ **Prayer Focus**—Blood

📖 **Scripture Inspiration**

But now in Christ Jesus you who once were far off have been brought near by the blood of Christ. (Ephesians 2:13 ESV)

◎ **Praying the Word**

Because of the blood You shed on the cross for me, Christ Jesus, I who was so far away have now been brought near to You.

❀ **Prayer Prompt**

O the blood of Jesus, that washes white as snow! Praise You, sweet Lamb of God, for the forgiveness, cleansing, and power that is in Your blood. Thank You that by it I may enter into the very Holy of Holies and be changed in the presence of God.

Prayer Focus_____

Scripture Inspiration

_____
_____
_____
_____

Praying the Word

_____
_____
_____
_____
_____
_____

Prayer Prompt

_____
_____
_____
_____
_____
_____
_____
_____
_____
_____

Day 17
Self

☕ **Prayer Focus**—Obedience

📖Scripture Inspiration

If you love me, obey my commandments. (John 14:15 NLT)

☉ Praying the Word

I do love You; help me to obey You.

✿ Prayer Prompt

I trust You, Lord. I know that anything You require of me is for my own good. I choose to obey You rather than myself or following after what others think I should do. I know there is safety, protection, and blessing in obeying Your commands. Help me to be quicker and quicker to obey You and show my deep love for You.

🍵 Prayer Focus _____

📖 Scripture Inspiration

_____

_____

_____

_____

🌀 Praying the Word

_____

_____

_____

_____

_____

_____

🌸 Prayer Prompt

_____

_____

_____

_____

_____

_____

_____

_____

_____

Day 17
Husband

📖**Scripture Inspiration**

A wise man will hear and increase learning, and a man of understanding will attain wise counsel. (Proverbs 1:5 NKJV)

☉ **Praying the Word**

Teach my husband to seek wise counsel, to hear it, understand it, and grow from it.

🦋 **Prayer Prompt**

You are the Wonderful Counselor. May my husband always seek You first when he is looking for wisdom. Surround him, also, with godly friends and role models who will speak the truth in love. Put an insatiable desire for wisdom in his heart that will perpetually keep him seeking after You. Thank You for Your promise to give wisdom to all who ask. Encourage my husband to be a seeker and an asker.

Prayer Focus_____

Scripture Inspiration

_____
_____
_____
_____

Praying the Word

_____
_____
_____
_____
_____
_____

Prayer Prompt

_____
_____
_____
_____
_____
_____
_____
_____
_____
_____

Day 17
Children

📖 Scripture Inspiration

Whoever walks with the wise becomes wise, but the companion of fools will suffer harm. (Proverbs 13:20 ESV)

☉ Praying the Word

Show my children the wisdom of walking with those who fear and respect You. Help them to see that even if they walk in righteousness, they can still suffer the collateral damage of hanging out with fools.

❀ Prayer Prompt

I am aware of how important my children's friends can be in their lives. I earnestly come to You and ask You to handpick the friends my children will have in every season of their lives. I take the authority that You have given me as their parent to draw a blood line around them to protect them from any unholy influences. Give them loyal, kind, wise, and godly friendships that will grow deeper as they grow older.

🍵 Prayer Focus _____

📖 Scripture Inspiration

_____

_____

_____

_____

🌀 Praying the Word

_____

_____

_____

_____

_____

_____

🌸 Prayer Prompt

_____

_____

_____

_____

_____

_____

_____

_____

_____

Day 17

Personal Influences

☕ **Prayer Focus**–Sick Friends

📖 **Scripture Inspiration**

Is anyone among you sick? Let him call for the elders of the church, and let them pray over him, anointing him with oil in the name of the Lord. (James 5:14 ESV)

🌀 **Praying the Word**

Lord, I lift up my friend _____ and ask You to touch her by Your Spirit and bring healing in the name of Jesus.

🌸 **Prayer Prompt**

Give me faith to believe Your promises of healing for my friends who are battling sickness. If You choose to answer in a way besides supernatural healing, remind us to trust in Your love and sovereignty.

Reaching Beyond

☕ **Prayer Focus**–Prayer Warriors

📖 **Scripture Inspiration**

I sought for a man among them who should build up the wall and stand in the breach before me for the land, that I should not destroy it, but I found none. (Ezekiel 22:30 ESV)

🌀 **Praying the Word**

Raise up men and women of prayer who will build a wall of protection and stand before You on behalf of our nation.

🌸 **Prayer Prompt**

Encourage those who tarry with You in prayer. Build their faith, fill them with Your spirit, and give them fresh vision.

Prayer Focus _____

Scripture Inspiration

_____
_____

Praying the Word

_____
_____

Prayer Prompt

_____
_____
_____

Prayer Focus _____

Scripture Inspiration

_____
_____

Praying the Word

_____
_____

Prayer Prompt

_____
_____
_____

Day 18

Praise

☕ **Prayer Focus**—Power

📖 **Scripture Inspiration**

Ah, Lord GOD! It is you who has made the heavens and the earth by your great power and by your outstretched arm! Nothing is too hard for you. (Jeremiah 32:17 ESV)

⊙ **Praying the Word**

I am addressing the Lord God! The One who made the heavens and the earth simply by His great power and outstretched arm. Nothing I bring to You in prayer is beyond Your ability to answer!

🌸 **Prayer Prompt**

I bow before You, aware of my smallness in light of Your greatness. You are awesome and mighty and able to create worlds with a word. I worship You, O powerful God. You are highly exalted, and it is my privilege to offer my simple praise.

Prayer Focus _____

Scripture Inspiration

_____
_____
_____
_____

Praying the Word

_____
_____
_____
_____
_____
_____

Prayer Prompt

_____
_____
_____
_____
_____
_____
_____
_____
_____
_____

Day 18

Self

Prayer Focus—God's Will

Scripture Inspiration

Your ears shall hear a word behind you, saying, "This is the way, walk in it," when you turn to the right or when you turn to the left. (Isaiah 30:21 ESV)

⊙ Praying the Word

Open my ears so I can hear You directing me which way I should go to find the center of Your will for my life.

🌸 Prayer Prompt

You are my Lord, and I submit my will to Yours. I know that it is only in staying within Your plans for my life that I will find the joy and satisfaction of discovering all You created me to be. Help me to discern and find Your will when I don't know which way to turn.

☕ Prayer Focus _____

📖 Scripture Inspiration

_____
_____
_____
_____

☺ Praying the Word

_____
_____
_____
_____
_____
_____

❀ Prayer Prompt

_____
_____
_____
_____
_____
_____
_____
_____
_____
_____

Day 18

Husband

☕ **Prayer Focus**—Peace

📖 **Scripture Inspiration**

Fear not, for I am with you; be not dismayed, for I am your God. I will strengthen you, yes, I will help you. I will uphold you with My righteous right hand. (Isaiah 41:10 NKJV)

◎ **Praying the Word**

Give my husband peace and a strong assurance that You will strengthen him and help him. Remind him not to be worried or afraid because You are not only the God, You are his God, and You will support him as he leans on You.

❀ **Prayer Prompt**

Relieve my husband of any anxiety that he carries with him. Remind him again of Your awesome power and love. Teach him to roll his burdens on to You so that he does not stress under the weight of his responsibilities. Give him sweet sleep and confident assurance that although he may not see how everything is going to work out, You have it all under control.

🍵 Prayer Focus _____

📖 Scripture Inspiration

_____

_____

_____

_____

🌀 Praying the Word

_____

_____

_____

_____

_____

_____

🌸 Prayer Prompt

_____

_____

_____

_____

_____

_____

_____

_____

_____

_____

Day 18
Children

☕ **Prayer Focus**—Diligence

📖 **Scripture Inspiration**

The plans of the diligent lead surely to plenty, but those of everyone who is hasty, surely to poverty. (Proverbs 21:5 NKJV)

ⓒ **Praying the Word**

Instruct my children on how to plan ahead and to work diligently so they may enjoy the abundance You desire to heap upon them. Help them to take their time in order to pursue excellence so they don't deprive themselves of Your blessings.

🌸 **Prayer Prompt**

Place within my children a strong work ethic. Give them a healthy pride in their work. Whatever their hands find to do, may they do it with all their might as an offering unto You. Because of their diligence and excellence, may they rise to the top in whatever situation You have them in. Teach them to follow through and care about the details, even if no one else sees but You.

🍵 Prayer Focus _____

📖 Scripture Inspiration

_____
_____
_____
_____

🌀 Praying the Word

_____
_____
_____
_____
_____
_____

🌸 Prayer Prompt

_____
_____
_____
_____
_____
_____
_____
_____
_____
_____

Day 18

Personal Influences

☕ **Prayer Focus**–Prayer Requests

📖 **Scripture Inspiration**

Ask, and it will be given to you; seek, and you will find; knock, and it will be opened to you. (Matthew 7:7 ESV)

☾ **Praying the Word**

Dear Lord, I'm knocking on the door of heaven, seeking You, and asking You to answer the following requests: _____

❀ **Prayer Prompt**

Thank You for not being so big that You don't care about every need and for not being too small to answer them all. I lift up these prayer requests and thank You in advance for answering them.

Reaching Beyond

☕ **Prayer Focus**–The Nations

📖 **Scripture Inspiration**

Be still, and know that I am God. I will be exalted among the nations, I will be exalted in the earth! (Psalm 46:10 ESV)

☾ **Praying the Word**

You are God, and beside You there is no other. Be lifted up so that all nations will worship You.

❀ **Prayer Prompt**

Almighty God, pour out Your grace, protection, and provision on the homes and families of each person on this planet. May they worship You as their Lord and Creator.

☕ Prayer Focus _____

📖 Scripture Inspiration

_____
_____

℗ Praying the Word

_____
_____

❀ Prayer Prompt

_____
_____
_____

☕ Prayer Focus _____

📖 Scripture Inspiration

_____
_____

℗ Praying the Word

_____
_____

❀ Prayer Prompt

_____
_____
_____

Day 19

Praise

☕ **Prayer Focus**—Hope

📖 **Scripture Inspiration**

May the God of hope fill you with all joy and peace in believing, so that by the power of the Holy Spirit you may abound in hope. (Romans 15:13 ESV)

☉ **Praying the Word**

Dear God of hope, please fill me with all joy and peace. Help me to believe, so that by the power of the Holy Spirit, I may grow ever more full of hope.

🌸 **Prayer Prompt**

My hope is in You, Lord. Even when I have lost hope in the things and people of this world, I am never without hope because I am never without You. Thank You for the plans You have for me, to give me a future and a hope. I will wait expectantly for Your promises to be fulfilled.

Prayer Focus_____

Scripture Inspiration

_____
_____
_____
_____

Praying the Word

_____
_____
_____
_____
_____

Prayer Prompt

_____
_____
_____
_____
_____
_____
_____
_____
_____

Day 19

Self

☕ **Prayer Focus**—Temptation

📖 Scripture Inspiration

But each one is tempted when he is drawn away by his own desires and enticed. Then, when desire has conceived, it gives birth to sin; and sin, when it is full-grown, brings forth death. (James 1:14–15 NKJV)

☺ Praying the Word

Lord, help me to fix my eyes and heart on You and Your Word so that I am so grounded in Truth that I'm not easily drawn away by my own selfish desires and lies from the enemy. Convict me of my unholy thoughts before they have a chance to become sin, which would only bring death to the good and godly plans You have for my life.

🌸 Prayer Prompt

I know that temptation isn't a sin, but I want to confess and bring my temptations into Your holy light, because I realize they can easily turn into sin if left in the dark. Please lead me not into temptation and deliver me from the evil one. I desire to do Your will, but I need Your strength when I am weak. Thank You for Your unconditional love.

🍵 Prayer Focus _____

📖 Scripture Inspiration

_____
_____
_____
_____

🌀 Praying the Word

_____
_____
_____
_____
_____

🌸 Prayer Prompt

_____
_____
_____
_____
_____
_____
_____
_____
_____

Day 19
Husband

📖 **Scripture Inspiration**

Let us consider how to stir up one another to love and good works, not neglecting to meet together, as is the habit of some, but encouraging one another. (Hebrews 10:24–25 ESV)

☉ **Praying the Word**

Refresh my husband through godly relationships. Remind him of the importance of meeting regularly with other believers to encourage each other and serve others.

🌸 **Prayer Prompt**

Strengthen the relationships in my husband's life that are ordained by You. I pray a special bond between my husband and all members of his family. Bring forgiveness, healing, and restoration to any broken relationships. If there is any person in my husband's life who is drawing him away from You, then I ask for an immediate severing of that relationship. Give him godly friendships with men who will encourage him in his walk with You.

Prayer Focus_____

Scripture Inspiration

_____
_____
_____
_____

Praying the Word

_____
_____
_____
_____
_____
_____

Prayer Prompt

_____
_____
_____
_____
_____
_____
_____
_____
_____

Day 19
Children

☕ **Prayer Focus**—Wisdom

📖 **Scripture Inspiration**

When wisdom enters your heart, and knowledge is pleasant to your soul, discretion will preserve you; understanding will keep you, to deliver you from the way of evil. (Proverbs 2:10–12 NKJV)

☺ **Praying the Word**

Dear Lord, fill my children's heart with Your wisdom. May they experience joy in the pursuit of knowledge. Give them good judgment and common sense to keep them from the paths of the evil one, and deliver them from temptation.

🌸 **Prayer Prompt**

I love the definition that wisdom is supernatural truth lived out in practical ways. Teach my children how to apply the wisdom in Your Word to every situation they encounter in life. I pray that they will walk in the knowledge that You are a practical God and that they would be cheating themselves if they kept You in a "Sunday box." Help me to train them to make asking for wisdom a daily—even moment-by-moment—habit.

Prayer Focus _____

Scripture Inspiration

_____
_____
_____
_____

Praying the Word

_____
_____
_____
_____
_____

Prayer Prompt

_____
_____
_____
_____
_____
_____
_____
_____
_____
_____

Day 19

Personal Influences

☕ **Prayer Focus**–Public Ministries

📖 **Scripture Inspiration**

Now to him who is able to keep you from stumbling and to present you blameless before the presence of his glory with great joy . . . be glory, majesty, dominion, and authority. (Jude 24–25 ESV)

🌀 **Praying the Word**

I ask that You keep _____ (public ministry) from stumbling, deliver them from the evil one, and allow them to bring You glory here on earth and eventually in heaven.

🦋 **Prayer Prompt**

I have personally been blessed by this ministry, and I want to offer something in return. So I lift up _____, asking You to pour out the treasures of heaven upon them.

Reaching Beyond

☕ **Prayer Focus**–Other Religions

📖 **Scripture Inspiration**

Jesus said to him, "I am the way, and the truth, and the life. No one comes to the Father except through me." (John 14:6 ESV)

🌀 **Praying the Word**

Open everyone's eyes to see that the Way to eternal life with the Father is through the truth of Jesus Christ.

🦋 **Prayer Prompt**

Have mercy on other religions that are looking in the wrong direction for reconciliation with You. Send Your Word and the revelation of the Holy Spirit to bring them to truth.

☕ Prayer Focus_____

📖 Scripture Inspiration

_____
_____

🌀 Praying the Word

_____
_____

🦋 Prayer Prompt

_____
_____
_____

☕ Prayer Focus_____

📖 Scripture Inspiration

_____
_____

🌀 Praying the Word

_____
_____

🦋 Prayer Prompt

_____
_____
_____

Day 20

Praise

☕ **Prayer Focus**—Coming Again

📖 **Scripture Inspiration**

*And if I go and prepare a place for you, I will come again
and receive you to Myself; that where I am, there you may be
also.* (John 14:3 NKJV)

☉ **Praying the Word**

Dear Jesus, You are, even now, preparing a place for me.
I cannot wait until You come again and take me unto
Yourself. I long to be with You.

❀ **Prayer Prompt**

Even so, come quickly, Lord Jesus! The promise of Your
sure return is almost more than I can even fathom. Thank
You that this world is not all that life is about. I am grateful
for the gift of life, but even more so for the gift of eternal
life with You! Help me to prepare for You and be ready
when You come to take me as Your bride. I love You.

☕ Prayer Focus_____

📖 Scripture Inspiration

_____
_____
_____
_____

☉ Praying the Word

_____
_____
_____
_____
_____
_____

❀ Prayer Prompt

_____
_____
_____
_____
_____
_____
_____
_____
_____

Day 20
Self

Prayer Focus—Finances

Scripture Inspiration

If you are untrustworthy about worldly wealth, who will trust you with the true riches of heaven? (Luke 16:11 NLT)

⊙ Praying the Word

I want You to be able to trust me with all that You have given us here on earth so You can depend on me for the really valuable blessings that are eternal.

❀ Prayer Prompt

First of all, thank You for supplying all our needs. My heart is to have a spirit of gratitude rather than the temptation to focus on wanting things I don't have. Provide all the resources we need to be able to pay our bills, and keep us from the temptation to go into debt. Give me discernment for how to be wise in spending and creative in saving.

Prayer Focus _____

Scripture Inspiration

_____

_____

_____

_____

Praying the Word

_____

_____

_____

_____

_____

Prayer Prompt

_____

_____

_____

_____

_____

_____

_____

_____

_____

Day 20

Husband

☕ **Prayer Focus**—Love

📖 **Scripture Inspiration**

You shall love the Lord your God with all your heart and with all your soul and with all your strength and with all your mind, and your neighbor as yourself. (Luke 10:27 ESV)

◎ **Praying the Word**

May my husband be so assured of Your love for him that his heart, soul, mind, and strength overflow with love for You and others.

❀ **Prayer Prompt**

Thank You, Jesus, that we can love You because You first loved us. Open my husband's heart to receive the fullness of that love and bask in it. Reveal a new facet of Your loveliness to him every day, so much so that he falls in love with You over and over again. Teach him how to give that love away to others.

☕ Prayer Focus _____

📖 Scripture Inspiration

_____
_____
_____
_____

☾ Praying the Word

_____
_____
_____
_____
_____

✿ Prayer Prompt

_____
_____
_____
_____
_____
_____
_____
_____
_____

Day 20
Children

☕ **Prayer Focus**—Forgiveness

📖 **Scripture Inspiration**

The discretion of a man makes him slow to anger, and his glory is to overlook a transgression. (Proverbs 19:11 NKJV)

☉ **Praying the Word**

Help my children to see the wisdom in not responding in the heat of the moment. May they reflect Your glory and overlook the faults of others just as You have overlooked their own sins.

❀ **Prayer Prompt**

Jesus, I pray that my children will walk freely in Your forgiveness and then extend that mercy to those around them. Help them to be quick to forgive those who have hurt them and to release them from any need to pay for the pain they have caused. Help my children to realize that forgiving someone doesn't make the other person right, but it does set their own heart free from any bitterness that could take root and choke the abundant life from them.

Prayer Focus _____

Scripture Inspiration

_____
_____
_____
_____

Praying the Word

_____
_____
_____
_____
_____

Prayer Prompt

_____
_____
_____
_____
_____
_____
_____
_____
_____

Day 20

Personal Influences

☕ **Prayer Focus**—Favorite Authors/Ministers

📖 **Scripture Inspiration**
Commit your work to the LORD, and your plans will be established.
(Proverbs 16:3 ESV)

🕉 **Praying the Word**
Lord, remind my favorite author/minister, _____, to
hand over any dreams and desires into Your care so Your plans
may be fulfilled for Your ministry.

🌸 **Prayer Prompt**
I pray that You will bless and multiply the ministry of _____
so that many other lives will be touched. As You expand his/her
influence, draw him/her closer to Your heart.

Reaching Beyond

☕ **Prayer Focus**—The Body of Christ

📖 **Scripture Inspiration**
We, though many, are one body in Christ, and individually members one of another. (Romans 12:5 ESV)

🕉 **Praying the Word**
With You as our Head, I ask You to knit us together as one body
so that we may work as a team to reveal Your glory.

🌸 **Prayer Prompt**
Purify and strengthen the body of Christ to walk in unity and
grace. Tear down walls and build bridges between us. Teach us
how to edify one another and build each other up.